LINCOLN ROAD TRIP

RED ⚡ LIGHTNING BOOKS

LINCOLN ROAD TRIP

THE BACK-ROADS GUIDE TO AMERICA'S FAVORITE PRESIDENT

JANE SIMON AMMESON

This book is a publication of

RED LIGHTNING BOOKS
1320 East 10th Street
Bloomington, Indiana 47405 USA

redlightningbooks.com

Manufactured in the United States of America

ISBN 978-1-68435-062-9
ISBN 978-1-68435-065-0

1 2 3 4 5 24 23 22 21 20 19

Contents

Preface and Acknowledgments

Though the largest and best-known place to explore Lincoln's history is Springfield, Illinois, where his home, law office, mausoleum, and other remnants of his life are well preserved, when I began my journey for this book I wanted to find Lincoln and his family off the well-traveled roads, on the backroads and byways where he lived most of his life before becoming president. Following Lincoln's footsteps meant spreading out large maps and pinpointing the interconnecting links that crisscross through Illinois, Indiana, Kentucky, Ohio, and even Michigan— though Lincoln seems to have made it there only once.

I am not a historian by training, but I love historical travel, and telling Lincoln's story as a journey is something I've always enjoyed, whether it's for magazines, newspapers, or travel apps, and getting to explore new "old" places has been a joy. In my wanderings, I've met people who were related to Lincoln's neighbors and even to Lincoln himself, such as Daryl Lovell, Barb and Jim Hevron, and Jerry Smith, who live in southwestern Indiana. Though no direct descendants survive (three of Mary and Abe Lincoln's four children died young), there are still family stories, passed down through generations, about Lincolns' time in the area. I've also met and befriended descendants of Lincoln's brother Josiah, who settled on the southeastern side of Indiana.

Much of the natural landscape, with its rolling hills and woodlands, seems not to have changed since Lincoln's time. Sure, there are no longer panthers, bears, or wolves, but its rural beauty endures. Many of the historic buildings from the time of Lincoln's youth remain as well. "When you touch this bannister," the guide says as I walk up the stairs of the Mary Todd Lincoln home in Lexington, Kentucky, "you're touching the same wood Abraham Lincoln once touched."

It's a simple sentence, but it still produces a thrill.

Though we know about many of the major events in Lincoln's life, there's controversy as well. Indeed, my good friend Mike Flannery, a longtime Chicago television political reporter, tells me more books have been written about Lincoln than anyone besides Jesus Christ. Real Lincoln historians spar over many aspects of his life, although I think they do all agree on the date of his death. When researching and writing this book, I often found well-respected scholars with conflicting information and interpretations. I've tried to use the most frequently report-ed "facts" and contemporary sources, although I understand that having something reported often doesn't mean it's true, and that even chroniclers of his day could and did misinterpret Lincoln or have their own agenda.

I'd like to point out that in this book I mention numerous in-cidents where settlers in the Lincoln/Boone families were killed by Indians—but it's important to note that settlers also killed a large number of Native Americans. In his book *The Wild Frontier: Atrocities during the American-Indian War from Jamestown Colony to Wounded Knee*, lawyer William M. Osborn attempted to list both alleged and actual atrocities in what would eventually be-come the United States. Starting from first contact in 1511 and ending in 1890, he documents the intentional and indiscrim-inate murder, torture, or mutilation of civilians, the wound-ed, and prisoners. His tally accounts for 7,193 people who died from monstrosities perpetrated by those of European descent and 9,156 people who died from atrocities committed by Native Americans. Of course, many attacks and murders were never recorded, and countless records have been lost to time. But Osborn's work indicates neither side was innocent of violent behavior.

Many of the people in Lincoln's early life were uneducated, and their spelling is irregular and characteristic of the time. In trying to keep the flavor of their written statements, I have kept their original spellings as well. Many newspapers in the early part of the 1800s used that old English spelling where the letter *s* in the middle of a word looks like an *f*. That I did change when necessary because it drove me crazy, and I figured it would drive readers just as crazy.

As for my own history writing this book and retracing Lincoln's life, I've had the wonderful support of so many people whose very hard work made all this possible. I owe a big thank-you to all of them. I hope I haven't left anyone out, but if I have, please forgive me.

Darlene Briscoe, descendant of Josiah Lincoln

Melissa Brockman, executive director, Spencer County Visitors Bureau

Mike Capps, chief of interpretation and resource management at Lincoln Boyhood National Memorial

Dixon Dedman, owner of the Beaumont Inn and distiller of Kentucky Owl

Megan Fernandez, descendant of Josiah Lincoln

Michael J. Flannery, Fox News-Chicago political anchor

Katie Fussenegger, CTP, CTIS, executive director, Shelby, Kentucky, Tourism & Visitors Bureau

Karen P. Hackett, executive director, Harrodsburg/Mercer County Tourist Commission

Niki Heichelbech-Goldey, director of communications, VisitLEX

Kathy Hertel-Baker, director of archives, Sisters of Charity of Nazareth

Jim and Barb Hevron, authors and historians

Joe Hevron, 1929–2011, avid Lincoln historian who worked at Holiday World for sixty-five years

Harold Holzer

Mike Kienzler, editor, SangamonLink.org, online encyclopedia of the Sangamon County Historical Society

Debbie Long, owner, Dudleys on Short

Daryl Lovell, author and historian

Pat Koch

Will Koch, 1961–2010, whom I will always remember and treasure—your love of Lincoln was sublime

Ouita Michel, executive chef, owner of Holly Hill

Jon Musgrave, author and historian

Natalie Partin, communications manager, Georgetown/Scott County Tourism

Carol Peachee, photographer and author of *Straight Bourbon: Distilling the Industry's Heritage*

Dawn Przystal, owner of Blue Elephant

Ruth Slottag, president, Sangamon County Historical Society

Jerry Smith, historian and member of the Broadwell family

Stephanie Tate, Alton Regional Convention and Visitors Bureau

Irene Tung, Quinn PR

Dan Usherwood, president of the Pleasant Plains Historical Society

Sheryl Vanderstel, food historian

Paula Werne, director of communications, Holiday World & Splashin' Safari (Koch Development Corporation)

Kathy Witt, sites director, Midwest Travel Journalists Association, Society of American Travel Writers, Authors Guild

And the biggest of thank-yous to Ashley Runyon, Peggy Solic, and Nancy Lightfoot at Indiana University Press for always being there for me. The same goes to my children, Evan and Nia. Love you!

Thank you,
Jane Simon Ammeson

LINCOLN
ROAD
TRIP

PROLOGUE

My friend Kathy Witt has set up a dinner for me at Eleanor Hamilton's Old Stone Tavern in Simpsonville, Kentucky, to meet Charlie Kramer, owner of Kentucky Back Roads. The tavern, which dates back to the 1700s, was likely another restaurant where Lincoln ate, and that's why I'm here—to enjoy the ambience of the thick stone walls, timbered ceilings, and the feel (yes, there's a feel) of the early 1800s, when horses and buggies passed by the front door and guests included tired travelers who had struggled along roads that were mostly covered in mud or dust, depending on the time of year. Kramer, who loves to joke and tell stories, tells me how Lincoln is buried just a few miles away.

Of course, my mind starts ruminating, running through my mental file of Lincoln lore. Is he referring, I wonder, to when

Lincoln's body was removed from its grave and hidden for years because of fears it would be stolen by grave robbers (a big "dirty" but money-making business back then)? I ask him, and Kramer laughs. "No, it's Lincoln's grandfather Captain Abraham Lincoln, who was killed by Indians. His nephew Mordecai managed to kill one of the attackers before he got him too."

President Lincoln's grandfather is buried nearby? I quickly look through all the Lincoln guides I carry with me. Not one mention.

"Where is it?" I ask.

He describes an out-of-the-way cemetery on a country road and then volunteers to take me after dinner. As if I could say no.

Turns out the Long Run Cemetery isn't far away but is not well marked, and it's getting dark when we finally find it. The gate looks locked. But never mind: further along part of the fencing has been torn down. Entering, we see a marker commemorating the Lincoln Tree, grown from an acorn from a spot in Albion, Illinois, where Lincoln campaigned for William Henry Harrison in 1840. The sign tells us that Captain Lincoln was killed near here in 1786.

Good—we're in the right place. But fifteen minutes later we're still looking. There's a sign commemorating the gravesite of President Harry Truman's great-uncle, and another for Richard Chenoweth, a founding father of Louisville, but nothing on Captain Lincoln. Are we in the wrong cemetery after all? Kramer pulls up an app and finds a photo of the tombstone. It's here, so we do another walk around—luckily, it's not a very big cemetery. We're just about to give up; we can't see, after all, with darkness starting to surround us. I'm walking past the foundation of an old church on my way back to the car when I look down. There's a marker here. It's not for Grandpa Lincoln, but right next to it is a newish gravestone reading:

In Memory of Abraham Linkhorn (Lincoln)
May 1738–May 1786
Paternal Grandfather of Abraham Lincoln, the Sixteenth
President of the United States

We've found it. It doesn't look like the photo Kramer pulled up on his phone, but it's definitely the right tombstone. Why isn't there a memorial marker? Kramer and I ask each other. And when did they put in a new stone?

The story of Captain Abraham Lincoln is an intriguing look into what life was like back then. In my journeys I discovered some of what I knew about President Lincoln wasn't totally true. I had thought Lincoln's family was poor, but many of his paternal relatives had been successful landowners, politicians, and businessmen, and his paternal grandmother also came from a prosperous family. Nor did I know that the Lincolns and the family of Daniel Boone were not only good friends and neighbors but had also intermarried across several generations. And although Nancy Hanks, the president's mother, was, as always touted, a loving mother, her family had a tendency toward illegitimate births. On the plus side, they can count Tom Hanks and George Clooney among their descendants.

I knew that the president's father, Tom Lincoln, and his family were frequently on the move: looking for better farmland, facing disappointment in legal battles over property rights, and escaping tragedies. But moving on was a Lincoln family trait. The original Lincolns had moved from England and then settled in various states back in the days when moving meant traveling by foot, wagon, horse, or flatboat in a time when roads were narrow traces carved through woods and meadows or, at best, "corduroys" made of logs and planks placed to keep travelers from being covered in dust or sinking into mud. Travelers found food and rest at stagecoach stops, several of which are still in business—which of course meant I had to stop there—or they would sleep on the ground or in the saddle.

THE NOON DAY INN

Over a half century ago, in 1963, a fierce wind ripped the weatherboards from the sides of the Log Inn in Warrenton, Indiana, revealing a wall made from rough-hewn poplar logs, twenty inches in diameter and held together by thick slabs of chinking. This was the wall of a twenty-by-thirty-foot room that old-timers had heard others even older talk about in a chain of stories going back generations and taking on the aura of myth. But it was true—this was a missing room where Lincoln dined in 1844. It's different from the other rooms of this bustling restaurant, where people often stand outside no matter the weather to get a seat and dine on Hoosier classics such as fried chicken, country ham, red cabbage, German potato salad, and mashed potatoes with milk gravy—dishes that Lincoln might have eaten when he returned to southwest Indiana for the first time since moving with his family to Illinois. Known as the Noon Day Inn in Lincoln's time, it was a stagecoach stop on the Evansville to Vincennes line and an established business, having opened in 1825.

Lincoln had been a poor, uneducated farm boy, tanner, ferryman, and store clerk before leaving Indiana. In the years that followed, he became a successful lawyer and politician; he'd married a wealthy Lexington belle whose family owned slaves, although they claimed to dislike slavery; and he now met and dined with friends and colleagues who lived in large, well-appointed homes and talked about politics and world affairs. He no longer had to get by on meager rations from what could be hunted that day, scratched from the family garden, or bartered for with other families. He had his own books instead of having to borrow.

But now he was back in Indiana campaigning for Henry Clay, a wealthy, sophisticated Lexington attorney and politician and a family friend of Mary Todd. The day he dined at the Noon Day Tavern, he would travel on to the home of William Jones, a successful businessman who had predicted Lincoln's success when he did odd jobs for him and clerked in his store. The Jones home is now a house museum; the replica of the cabin where Lincoln lived is only a few miles but a million lifestyles away. Lincoln also stopped at the gravesites of his mother, Nancy

Hanks Lincoln, his sister, Sarah Lincoln Grigsby, and Sarah's baby boy. They all were buried in Little Pigeon Creek where the Lincolns had lived.

It would be the first and last time Lincoln returned to this part of the state where he had lived his formative years in what is now Spencer County, Indiana.

FOLLOWING LINCOLN

Visiting the cabins where Lincoln was born and where he lived in Kentucky, Indiana, and Illinois (all reproductions based on descriptions) and then touring the homes of friends he made as he became a successful lawyer and politician, such as the Elihu B. Washburne House, a one-and-a-half-story Greek Revival house with tall white pillars located in historic Galena, Illinois, shows how remarkable his rise in the world was.

It was Washburne who, hearing from the Pinkertons of a possible assassination attempt when Lincoln arrived on the 6:00 a.m. train on February 23, 1861, rode to the station in his carriage and took Lincoln to the Willard Hotel, where he was to give a speech. Consider that, as a youth, Lincoln had walked miles and miles to the Spencer County Courthouse in Rockport or the Warrick County Courthouse in Boonville, because he often didn't have a horse to ride.

As Lincoln prospered, he must also have marveled at the difference between his gracious surroundings and the three-sided cabin where he and his family lived their first month or so in Little Pigeon Creek in southwestern Indiana. He'd grown up eating game, including raccoon, said to be among his favorites. His wife, a pretty belle, had lived in Lexington, called the Athens of the West, in a finely furnished home staffed by slaves, where the dining room table groaned with hams, buttered biscuits, fried chickens, and rich cakes.

Lexington today is a beautiful city with many remaining early nineteenth-century buildings that often tell the story of the conflicted nature of the War between the States. In lovely Gratz Park, next to the campus of Transylvania University, the home of Confederate General John Hunt Morgan, leader of Morgan's Raiders, sits across the green from the Bodley-Bullock House, which served as Union headquarters during the Civil War. As an example of Kentucky courtliness, it's said that when Mrs. Hunt was surrounded by an angry mob while shopping at the farmers' market during the war, Mr. Bullock kindly escorted her to safety. The Morgan home and its stately gardens look down on the former law offices of Kentucky legislator and statesman Henry Clay. Clay's spectacular eighteen-room Ashland estate, situated not far from his office in one of Lexington's elegant historic districts, is now open to the public, as is the house where Mary Todd Lincoln grew up.

The conflict engendered by the Civil War was also played out among those who did or did not vote for Lincoln, including his own family members and former neighbors. According to Hevron family lore, though the Gentry and Romine families were good friends of Abraham Lincoln, none of them voted for him when he ran for president of the United States because he ran on the wrong ticket: Republican.

Lincoln's father, Thomas Lincoln, was also antislavery and his reasoning reflects some of the issues that impact us today in our global economy. When people owned slaves that meant less work for hardworking men and women who earned wages. In a global environment, countries that don't follow environmental rules and where workers earn a pittance mean fewer jobs in countries that steward the environment and take care of their workers.

Journeying with Lincoln is learning. Sure, we know about the log cabin—and, my goodness, the replicas such as those at Lincoln Pioneer Village and the Lincoln National Boyhood Memorial are cozy looking, clean, and neat, with the smell of baking bread emanating from a pioneer kitchen and, depending on the season, pretty flowers blooming in the yard or snow gently falling on split rail fences.

But the real log cabins usually had a single door and at best a window or two—without glass. It was one-room living: Kitchen, beds, and living area were all heated by the fireplace where the cooking took place in a large iron pot hanging above the flames. Bathroom needs were attended to either outdoors or in a chamber pot. Privacy was nonexistent. While Nancy Lincoln lay dying, in pain and suffering, her family was just steps away, eating their dinner, studying, or working on projects.

People have debated for more than 150 years about how Lincoln became such a great man. He gives us a hint in a letter he wrote to his cousin Jesse Lincoln in 1854 about the death of his grandfather: "The story of his death by the Indians, and of Uncle Mordecai, then fourteen years old, killing one of the Indians, is the legend more strongly than all others imprinted upon my mind and memory." Captain Abraham Lincoln's death was a defining moment, one with repercussions throughout the decades, as we'll talk about more in this book. Tragedy followed Lincoln throughout his life, but he did not allow his losses or bouts of depression to prevent him from accomplishing great things—the greatest being granting freedom to four million slaves.

We can never meet Abraham Lincoln or speak to him or those he knew and loved. We'll never walk alongside him for seventeen miles to listen to court cases in Spencer County, Indiana; paddle a canoe down the Sangamon River on our way to New Salem, Illinois; or dine with his family when he was a young boy at the Old Talbott Tavern in Kentucky as they awaited a court verdict that eventually took their home away from them. We'll never hear the panthers scream at night, see the bright yellow eyes of the wolves staring at us in the Indiana darkness, or trudge with Lincoln through a deep winter snow on his way to see a girl who had caught his eye. But we can follow the byways and back roads that he followed as a way of connecting across the decades to the times and places that made Lincoln the man he became.

IN THE BEGINNING

The Lincoln Heritage

With the crack of a rifle shot, eleven-year-old Josiah saw his father, mortally wounded, fall to the ground where they'd just been planting corn. Josiah took off running toward Hughes Station, the rudimentary fort his father had helped build when the family moved to Kentucky two years earlier. Just as quick to act, fourteen-year-old Mordecai ran into the family's cabin and grabbed the gun he knew was there. Thomas, only about eight, started crying as he stood by his father's body. Fearing Thomas would be killed and his father scalped, Mordecai acted decisively. Looking through the loose cracks of the log cabin and seeing the murderer—a Native American wearing a large silver pendant stolen from another farmer—he aimed and pulled the trigger. It was a direct hit. Mordecai had avenged the death of his father, Captain Abraham Lincoln.

LOUISVILLE, KENTUCKY

Long Run Cemetery

Tucked along a country lane near Eastwood, Kentucky, Long Run Cemetery is easy to miss at first. The only clue to this being more than an old, half-forgotten country cemetery is a sign saying that the large oak tree shading the wrought-iron gate grew out of an acorn from an oak in Albion, Illinois, under which Abraham Lincoln gave a great speech in 1844. Someone has taken care to erect markers touting the accomplishments of several people buried here. None refer to the president's grandfather. Ringing the interior of the old burial ground are the stone foundations of the original Long Run Baptist Church, which Abraham Lincoln helped build. Near here, within a few feet of the foundations, I find the tombstone for Abraham Linkhorn (Lincoln to you and me). There are no other family members nearby. After Lincoln was shot, they all moved away, so he rests alone.

Two Hundred Years of Travelers

Just seven miles from Long Run Cemetery, going south on the wonderfully named Old Stage Coach Road to US 60 East, is Eleanor Hamilton's Old Stone Inn in Simpsonville, Kentucky. Built in the early 1800s, with two-foot-thick stone walls and large-planked wooden floors, each room has a fireplace, for how else would you keep warm on cold days and nights? The inn was a stagecoach stop, tavern, and hostel along the Midland Trail. President Andrew Jackson stayed here as he traveled between Tennessee and Washington, DC. Logic and oral history say that when Abraham Lincoln was a successful attorney and statesman he was a visitor there as well. "People, especially the old-timers, tell stories about him being here," says Christopher Kayrouz, owner of the inn. It's also possible that Lincoln might have stopped by to visit his grandfather's grave. For those tracing Lincoln's heritage in Kentucky, the area east of Louisville is

Tradition states that Captain Abraham Linkhorn (Lincoln), President Abraham Lincoln's paternal grandfather, was buried by his cabin. A headstone memorializing the captain was placed in the Long Run Baptist Church Cemetery in 1937 and remains today near the foundation of the church. The church and cemetery were added to the National Register of Historic Places in 1975. *Photo courtesy of Jane Simon Ammeson*

the beginning of his family history here and thus the first stop on any trip through the Bluegrass State.

Captain Abraham Lincoln was just forty-six when he died in 1786 on the large parcel of land he'd purchased in 1780 in what would become eastern Jefferson County, about twenty miles from downtown Louisville. In 1782 he and his family had moved from Virginia and settled on "the Fork of Floyd's Fork" (now Long Run). At that time battles between pioneers and Native Americans, who rightly considered the land their own, were fierce and bloody in this part of Kentucky. To protect themselves, pioneers erected "stations" or wooden stockades, usually located near a spring to ensure a supply of water, and typically named after the first white settler to arrive.

Abraham Lincoln had no chance to seek shelter in nearby Hughes Station when he was shot dead in his cornfield. Besides his three sons, he left a widow, Bathsheba, and two daughters,

Once a stagecoach stop, the Old Stone Inn may have been a place where Lincoln visited while journeying through Kentucky. It is not far from his grandparents' homestead and where his grandfather, Captain Abraham Lincoln, is buried. *Photo courtesy of Jane Simon Ammeson*

The interior of the Old Stone Inn with its solid stone walls, planked-wood floors, and fireplaces gives the feel of what it must have been like two hundred years ago.

Nancy and Mary. A younger daughter, Abigail, born in 1782, appears to have died by the time of Captain Lincoln's death. His estate included 5,544 acres of prime Kentucky land, and it would have provided all of his children a very comfortable living. But because of the law of primogeniture, Mordecai inherited the majority of his father's estate. Bathsheba got a small share; the other children received little or nothing.

An English hereditary law, primogeniture was developed as a way to keep estates in the hands of one person, so they could be passed down in their entirety across the generations instead of being dissipated and spread too thin. If the oldest son died, the estate went to the next oldest male, and so on. Because a woman, even a wife, could not inherit the estate, if no sons survived, it passed to the nearest male descendent, sometimes someone unknown to the family. A widow and her children could be turned out of their home by a second nephew or some other obscure heir. For Captain Lincoln's younger sons, Josiah and Thomas Lincoln, primogeniture meant they would have to make their own way in the world. For Bathsheba, it meant she would never seem to have a home of her own again and was left to raise five children all by herself.

Bathsheba's husband had moved her into the wilds of Kentucky and then left her on her own, but it wasn't as if she hadn't been warned.

According to the members of the Herring family still living in the Shenandoah Valley, as reported by one of them to Mr. Lea in 1908, "Abraham Lincoln, who married Bathsheba Herring, was a poor and rather plain man. Her aristocratic father looked with scorn on the alliance and gave his daughter the choice of giving up her lover or being disinherited. The high-spirited young woman did not hesitate. She married the man she loved and went with him to the savage wilds of Kentucky in 1782. Her husband was afterwards killed by an Indian, and one of her sons, a lad of 12 years, killed the Indian, avenging his father's death. Bathsheba Herring Lincoln was a woman of fine intelligence and strong character. She was greatly loved and respected by all who knew her." (Ida M. Tarbell, *In the Footsteps of the Lincolns*, 55)

Always Moving On

Captain Lincoln's youngest son and the future president's father, Thomas Lincoln moved many times over the years, both as a child and as a grown man—sometimes from necessity, such as when he lost his farm because of legal issues with the title, and other times trying for a better life for his family. He wasn't the only Lincoln who didn't seem to think twice about packing up and hitting the road. Starting with family members who moved to America in the 1700s, the Lincolns would settle temporarily and then, despite seeming prosperity, would journey on, at times on their own but often in conjunction with the Boone family.

It would take another book just to keep track of these two families' peregrinations. I'll make it easy and start with chronicling Captain Abraham Lincoln's major moves. Captain Abe (he received his title fighting in the Revolutionary War) and his family were neighbors and relatives by marriage of the Boones in Berks County, Pennsylvania. When the Boones moved from Pennsylvania to North Carolina and then on to settle in Virginia, the Lincolns left to join them.

In May 1769, while still living in North Carolina, Daniel Boone and a small group of men began an exploration west. Years later Boone would write, with the help of a friend,

> We proceeded successfully; and after a long and fatiguing journey through a mountainous wilderness, in a westward direction, on the seventh day of June following we found ourselves on Red River, where John Finley had formerly gone trading with the Indians; and, from the top of an eminence, saw with pleasure the beautiful level of Kentucky. . . .
>
> We found everywhere abundance of wild beasts of all sorts, through this vast forest. The buffalo were more frequent than I have seen cattle in the settlements, browsing on the leaves of the cane, or cropping the herbage on those extensive plains, fearless, because ignorant, of the violence of man. Sometimes we saw hundreds in a drove, and the numbers about the salt springs were amazing. (Gilbert Imlay, *A Topographical Description of the Western Territory of North America*, 339)

To Boone, Kentucky was a paradise and he resolved to move his family there. After listening to descriptions like this and hearing Boone say, "Heaven must be a Kentucky kind of place," of course the Lincolns would follow. And so off they all eventually went.

SPRINGFIELD, KENTUCKY

As we know, settling on Floyd's Fork would be the last earthly move for the captain, but his widow, Bathsheba, moved several more times during her long life, mostly living with relatives, as her husband's death had left her in a precarious financial position. Her children accompanied her until they grew up and married. Moving in with relatives was the norm in early pioneer days, even when a typical home was a one-room log cabin, only sometimes with an upper loft area. There often seemed to be an overabundance of aunts, uncles, elderly parents, cousins, neighborhood orphans, nieces, and nephews living together.

Bathsheba's first move after Captain Lincoln's death was to Springfield, Kentucky. It couldn't have been an easy trip for Bathsheba and her brood. Though the trip from Long Run to Springfield south on KY 555 takes me a little over an hour, those fifty-four miles in Bathsheba's time most likely took a couple of days, loaded down as she was with children and furniture.

In Springfield, I visit the Lincoln Homestead State Park, which houses re-creations of the 1782 cabin and blacksmith shop where Tom Lincoln spent his youth and learned a trade. It's an interesting piece of history, but what is more amazing is the juxtaposition of the raw living and working conditions of Thomas with those of his oldest brother, Mordecai, who lived in comparative pioneer splendor, emphasizing again the impact Abraham Lincoln's early death would have on the lives of his sons. Mordecai would become a landed gentleman and breed racehorses, while Tom could barely afford an old nag to carry sacks of grain to the mill.

Mord

After coming of age and collecting his inheritance, Mord (as Mordecai was called) married Mary Mudd. The two built a two-story cabin and had six children, including another Mordecai. Pioneer families often used the same first names in each succeeding generation, which was a good way to honor ancestors, but is really a pain for genealogists and historians.

Mord and Mary's cabin was enlarged and its facade enhanced by its second owner. Now listed on the National Register of Historic Places, the Mordecai Lincoln Homestead is located about a mile from the main visitor center at the Lincoln Homestead State Park. It is the only existing structure owned and occupied by a member of the Lincoln family in Kentucky still standing on its original site.

Lincoln resembled his Uncle Mord physically, and both were known for their wit, common sense, storytelling ability, and compassion. A less favorable family trait that affected both uncle and nephew was a strong tendency toward melancholy. Lincoln often told people that his intelligent, humorous, and talented uncle influenced him greatly, adding that "Uncle Mord had run off with all the talents of the family."

In a strange twist of history, Mary Mudd Lincoln was a first cousin twice removed of Dr. Samuel A. Mudd, who treated John Wilkes Booth for the wound he received during his escape after shooting President Lincoln at Ford's Theater. Having failed to report the incident for twenty-four hours, Mudd was tried as a conspirator in the president's murder. Luckily for the doctor, he escaped the death penalty by one vote and instead was sentenced to life in prison. President Andrew Johnson, Lincoln's successor, pardoned the doctor in 1869, in part because he helped stem an outbreak of yellow fever while imprisoned in Florida. Before his trial and conviction, Samuel and his wife had produced four children. After his release, they added five more to their brood. Imagine how many more they might have had if he hadn't spent those years in jail. That poor woman got a lucky break.

The Future Mrs. Thomas Lincoln

Springfield would be the nexus for many happenings in the Lincoln family, but most important, it was where Thomas would meet his future wife Nancy Hanks—entranced, it is said, by her ability to spin thread. Nancy had come from Virginia and was living near Springfield, Kentucky, with Richard Berry Sr., who was married to Rachel Shipley Berry, the sister of Nancy's mother, Lucy Shipley. Their home, now called the Francis Berry House, is where Tom Lincoln, then living in Elizabethtown, proposed to Nancy. It is also now on the grounds of Lincoln Homestead State Park in Springfield, having been moved in 1941 from where it originally stood about a mile away. The two-story log cabin is decidedly more upscale than the one-room cabins Nancy would live in after marrying Thomas. The exterior logs and some of the furnishings are original, and Nancy's upstairs bedroom (yes, she had a bedroom though we're not sure how many people she shared it with) looks cozy and comfortable.

Family Scandals

Pioneer life was in many ways just as undisciplined as our own times, as the lifestyles and rumors about the Lincoln and Hanks families show. For those who consider our era morally corrupt compared to the good old days, consider the history of the Hanks women, who it seems, might have been somewhat overexuberant when it came to premarital sex. Nancy Hanks Lincoln's sister Sarah or Polly Hanks never married although she had six children, all of whom grew to maturity and bore their mother's last name. One of those children was Sophie Hanks, who, after her mother died, came to live for a time with Nancy and Tom after they moved to Indiana.

Nancy Hanks Lincoln was an excellent seamstress and fantastic mother; of that we have no doubt. But it seems she may also have been, as they said back then, born on the wrong side of the blanket. Whatever. I don't care. But I'm always willing to pass on gossip. Nancy's ancestry is very complex, and DNA testing is still trying to sort it all out. It appears that her mother was probably Lucy Hanks—there's some dispute about that, but it's so complicated that you'll have to trust us on that. Lucy wasn't married when Nancy was born, and her father may have been either James Hanks or Henry Sparrow—although other names are suggested as well. Lucy eventually married Henry Sparrow, but only after she faced "fornication" charges. Sparrow was a reverend and Lucy his housekeeper, and, well, you know, people will talk. So in November 1789, a grand jury of twelve men (remember, women couldn't vote back then, nor could they serve on juries) convened to take up charges against Lucy. Interestingly no one filed similar charges against Sparrow. Anyway, he decided to do the right thing and the couple took out a marriage license on April 26, 1790, married a week later, and on May 25, 1790, an order was entered to discontinue the case. But Lucy was never cleared of the charges in her lifetime, or indeed for over a century, until two attorneys decided to rectify that.

Lincoln's Grandmother
Suit Filed to Clear Lucy Hanks's Name

Advocate-Messenger, Danville, KY, Thursday, September 9, 1976
    An effort is being made in Mercer Circuit Court to purge the name of Abraham Lincoln's grandmother, Lucy Hanks, who was accused of fornication in 1789.
    A suit styled Commonwealth of Kentucky vs. Lucy Hanks has been filed by Attorney James A. Peterson, a historian of White Oaks Spring Farm, Yorkville, IL, and by local Attorney David Taylor, as friends of the Court and on behalf of the heirs of Lucy Hanks.

Who's Your Daddy?

As for whether James Hanks or Henry Sparrow was Nancy's father, though history knows her as Hanks, Sparrow was the last name she often used of at that time of her life. More speculatively, some historians claim that Abraham Lincoln wasn't

Tom's son but instead was fathered by a man with the last name of Enlow or Enloe. There were Enlows who were friends of the Lincolns and who also moved to southwestern Indiana, where they owned the Enlow Mill in Jasper. Mrs. Enlow was said to have helped deliver Abraham while they still lived in Kentucky. If he truly were her husband's child, that seems mighty nice of her.

Even Abe seemed unsure of his heritage. According to William Herndon, Lincoln's law partner and biographer, Lincoln told him his maternal grandfather was "a well-bred Virginia farmer or planter." I told you it was complicated.

So much of what we know of pioneer life is from movies and TV shows, but it was really a much more nuanced time as the following article, dating back almost 150 years, shows.

The Indiana Herald
Huntington Indiana
Wednesday, March 18, 1874
In the year 1859, I went to Springfield, Kentucky to teach and was in that neighborhood when Abraham Lincoln received the nomination for president. On the announcement of the name of the candidate a farmer remarked that "you should not be surprised if this were a son of Thomas Lincoln and Nancy Hanks who were married at the house of Uncle Frank Berry." (the old house is still standing)

A few days later I visited an aged lady by the name of Litsey, who interested me much by giving a description of the wedding of the father and mother of the new candidate; she having been a friend of the bride and present at the wedding. In 1866 after the liberation of 4 million slaves had made the name of Abraham Lincoln memorable, I was again in the neighborhood and visited the old home, now historic, in which were celebrated the nuptial rights referred to above.

Its surroundings are among the most picturesque in Kentucky. The Beech Fork, a small river of wonderful meanderings, flows near, and is lost to view in a semi-circular amphitheater of hills. As I remember the story of Nancy Hanks, it ran thus. Her father and mother were Virginians and died when she was young; her mother's name was Shipley and she is known to have had two sisters, one of whom married a man by the name of Berry, and the other, Robert Mitchell, who came to Kentucky about the year 1789. While on the journey, this family was set upon by the Indians and Mrs. M. fatally wounded, and their only daughter, Sarah, a child of 11, was captured and carried away. Mr. Mitchell bore his dying wife to Crab Orchard and like Abraham of old, purchased that renowned spot for the burial place of his wife. After the last sad rites, he mounted his horse, accompanied by his friend, Gen. Adair and went in search of his daughter, but was drowned in Dick's River while attempting to cross.

C.C.H.V.

For those wondering about poor Sarah, now an orphan and captive of the Indians, shortly after "Mad Anthony" Wayne's Treaty of the Timbers with the Indians in 1794, she was rescued and went to live in the Berry home where Nancy was residing. The two became good friends and Nancy, who was a whiz with a spinning wheel, taught Sarah what was described even then as the "lost art" of spinning.

C.C.H.V., whose full name we don't know, also offered a description of what convinced Thomas that Nancy would make an excellent wife.

It was the custom in those days to have spinning parties, on which occasions the wheels of the ladies were carried to the house designated, to which the competitors came distaff in hand, ready for the work of the day. At a given hour, the wheels were put in motion and the filmy fiber took the form of firmly lengthened strand in their mystic hands, fence strand in their mental hand.

Tradition says Nancy bore the palm using the finest and longest threads. Mr. Lincoln was not an exception to the rule for great men which requires that their mother shall be talented. Thomas Lincoln came, it is believed, into the neighborhood to visit his brother Mordicai, who lived near Major Berry, and there learned of the skill of Nancy.

As Ulysses, he was ambitious and became the husband of Nancy, whose thread of gold has been woven into the warp and woof of the National Constitution.

Once married, Thomas and Nancy settled at Mill Creek, where their first child, Sarah, was born. They then moved on to Sinking Spring Farm near Hodgenville, so called because of the spring that bubbled up from the bottom of a deep cave. The spring still bubbles inside a cool cavern, but the home must have been a disappointment to Nancy. We're only saying this based upon our own materialistic values, but really, does any gal desire a place with a glassless window covered in greased paper or by a thin piece of animal skin and a single door to the outside attached by leather hinges? Oh, and need I add that the floor was hard-packed dirt?

HODGENVILLE, KENTUCKY: LINCOLN'S BIRTHPLACE

I was born February 12, 1809, in then Hardin County, Kentucky, at a point within the now county of Larue, a mile or a mile and a half from where Hodgen's mill now is. My parents being dead, and my memory not serving, I know no means of identifying the precise locality. It was on Nolen Creek.

A. Lincoln.

June 14, 1860.

After Lincoln's death, historians discovered the land where he had been born, and, like the ever-moving Lincoln family, a re-created cabin said to be his birth cabin, too, hit the road. Disassembled, the logs were shipped to Chicago, reconstructed, and exhibited at the World's Columbian Exposition in 1893 before going on tour throughout the United States.

When the tour was over, the logs were returned to their original site, put back together, and then encased in an outer building made of marble, ensuring that the cabin would withstand the ages. It is now part of the 116-acre Abraham Lincoln Birthplace National Historical Park in Hodgenville, about thirty-seven miles west of Springfield—more than a long day's travel back in the day of Tom and Nancy but just over thirty minutes for me.

The sixteen-by-eighteen-foot cabin was built from about 143 oak and chestnut logs chinked together with clay. The roof was covered with rough wooden shingles and had a small, box-like stick-and-clay chimney. Other amenities, as today's real estate ads say, included a stone fireplace. Little of the surrounding landscape has changed from when the Lincolns lived there, and park activities are designed to let visitors view and experience the hard chores of pioneer life, including rail splitting. Life-sized bronze statues of the family are poised at the entrance of the park's museum.

KNOB CREEK, KENTUCKY: LINCOLN'S BOYHOOD HOME

Tom and Nancy had worked hard to buy Sinking Spring Farm, but because of Kentucky's then byzantine land-title problems, they lost the land and the family was forced to hit the road again, moving on in 1811 to what is now Abraham Lincoln's Boyhood Home at Knob Creek, just northeast of Hodgenville. This is easily reached by taking Kentucky 210 north into Hodgenville and then following US 31 east. Lincoln was two and a half at the time of the move, and in a widely quoted 1860 letter to Samuel Haycraft of Elizabethtown, he wrote "My earliest recollection is of the Knob Creek place."

Nancy had her last child, named Thomas, at the Knob Creek farm; sadly he died shortly after birth. Sarah and Abe attended a subscription school in the area (Kentucky didn't have public schools until 1830). Kentucky Historical Marker #1482 identifies the approximate site of Abraham Lincoln's first school, a very short drive from Knob Creek now, but the two Lincoln children had to make their way through a heavily forested area. The marker reads as follows:

The Memorial Building at the Abraham Lincoln Birthplace National Park was built in 1909–1911 on the site where Lincoln was born and houses a "symbolic" Lincoln birth cabin. *Photo courtesy of Wikimedia*

Abraham Lincoln's First School

Lincoln's formal education began in a primitive log cabin near this site. While the Lincoln family was living on Knob Creek, he and his sister Sarah attended ABC schools for a short period of time. The first school was taught by Zachariah Riney; the second by Caleb Hazel. The Lincolns' home stood two miles south on the old Cumberland Road.

It was here at Knob Creek that Lincoln first saw slavery up close when he spied African-Americans being marched south along the Bardstown–Green River Turnpike, part of the old Cumberland Road, to be sold as slaves. When Abe was seven, in

1816, the Lincolns lost a legal battle against a consortium who claimed they owned ten thousand acres (including the Lincolns' thirty acres) in Knob Creek, and the family was forced to move on again.

ELIZABETHTOWN, KENTUCKY

Bathsheba's Later Years

While her children were moving and raising families, Lincoln's paternal grandmother, Bathsheba, had eventually settled in Elizabethtown, a charming city just twenty-one miles from Abraham Lincoln's Boyhood Home at Knob Creek via KY 210. Her home is gone, but the mantelpiece is on display at the Lincoln Room of the Fort Knox Saber & Quill, a dining room open to the public in Elizabethtown. As was unfortunately common back then, only two of Bathsheba's children would survive her.

Mord's death was reflective of the pioneer life and just as atypical of how people die today as his father being shot by an Indian. Mordecai and his family, including four of his children, had moved from Kentucky to Fountain Park (now Fountain Green), Illinois, in 1828. In December 1830, a blizzard roared through the region while Mordecai was away from home, and although his horse returned to the family homestead, Mord did not. Whether he fell and couldn't get back on his horse and froze to death, or whether he had a heart attack or some other injury that kept him from staying in the saddle and riding home was never determined. Twenty feet of snow covered Mordecai's body, and it wasn't discovered until the spring thaw the following April.

Bathsheba's daughter Mary Ada Lincoln was first the common-law wife of Daniel Edgar Crume, who died in 1824. Their relationship is described as beginning after the death of Daniel's first wife around 1791 and ending before 1801. The couple had two daughters, both of whom died before 1880. In 1801, Mary married Ralph Crume, who was Daniel Crume's nephew, and they had three children. Mary Lincoln Crume is believed to have died between 1830 and 1832 and is buried in the Crume family cemetery in Crume Valley, Breckinridge County, Kentucky.

By 1835, Bathsheba's son Josiah was also dead. Her daughter Nancy would live until 1843. It was Thomas who lived the longest, dying in 1851. When she died in 1836, Bathsheba wasn't buried with her husband, and like her husband, her gravesite fell into disrepair.

On February 15, 1931, the *Courier Journal* published a photo showing several tottering tombstones in a neglected cemetery overgrown with weeds and shrubs. The photo was accompanied by the following caption.

> The small neglected stone at the right is the grave of Bathsheba Lincoln, the grandmother of President Lincoln, and the two at the left are those of Mary Brumfield Crume and (her mother) Nancy Lincoln Brumfield (far left), resp. first cousin and aunt of President Lincoln.

That article spurred action, and Bathsheba's gravesite and that of her daughter Nancy Lincoln Brumfield are now located at Fort Knox in an area not open to the public.

The history of the Civil War is even more closely entwined with the history of the Lincolns than with most families of that era, and the convergence of the events of the war and of the family is evident everywhere in and around Elizabethtown, the seat of Hardin County. Fort Knox is Kentucky's largest and best preserved earthen Civil War fort, and costumed interpreters there host living-history and reenactment events throughout the year. The Hardin County History Museum has collected an amazing amount of material associated with Fort Sands, Fort Boyle, and Fort Duffield—all Civil War forts located within the county. These include training manuals, photos, and a telegraph dispatch from President Lincoln to Union general Rousseau while Rousseau was stationed at Camp Nevin, a training camp in Nolin, south of Elizabethtown, that housed approximately fifteen thousand troops between October 1861 and January 1862.

The Lincoln Museum and Boundary Oak Distillery

In Kentucky, both bourbon and history are always in play, and at the Boundary Oak Distillery in Radcliff, just northeast of Elizabethtown, master distiller Brent Goodin covered these two basics when he created Lincoln Spirits. This limited-edition bourbon uses corks made from the Boundary Oak tree, which was used as one of the boundary markers on the farm where Lincoln was born and is thought to have been the last living link to Lincoln when it died in 1976. It was quite the tree too—standing ninety feet high, with a trunk diameter of six feet and a crown spread of one hundred and fifteen feet. Boundary Oak Distillery obtained some of the wood, but most of it was preserved by the Lincoln Museum in the Hodgenville National Historic District. Boundary Oak wood from the museum has been used to make gavels distributed to dignitaries from Supreme Court justices to state governors and foreign leaders. Featuring period artifacts, a series of dioramas of Lincoln's life, and a collection of wax figures of historic people, the Lincoln Museum is three miles north of the Abraham Lincoln Birthplace National Historical Park and seven miles west of Lincoln's Boyhood Home at Knob Creek.

As for the bourbon, Boundary Oak's Lincoln Spirits is not to be taken lightly. At an auction for the first bottle, held before it was even ready to be released, the top bid was over $28,000, the highest price ever paid for a bottle of American whiskey. When you buy a bottle, you also get a copy of Lincoln's liquor license (he is the only president to have had one).

In another interesting tie-in with history, a relative of distillery owner Brent Goodin established a fort at what is now Bardstown, where you can also find the Women's Civil War Museum and Old Bardstown Village and Civil War Museum. If you're already visiting Bardstown, it's only twenty-four miles on

KY 62/Lincoln Parkway and Patriot Parkway to get to Radcliff to sample some bourbons—and no, there won't be any free samples of Lincoln Spirits.

Wanted: A New Wife

After losing their home on Knob Creek, Nancy and Thomas moved to Indiana, settling on Little Pigeon Creek. In 1818 Nancy died, and Thomas, needing another wife, returned to Elizabethtown and proposed marriage to Sarah Bush Johnston. He'd pursued her before marrying Nancy, but she had turned him down and married Daniel Johnston instead.

One of nine children born into a prosperous family, Sarah was fond of the latest styles and had blue-gray eyes and a light complexion. She was described as proud, energetic, hard-working, neat, and possessing good sense. Though she supposedly declined Thomas because she didn't think he'd amount to much, Daniel wasn't much of a winner either, and his brothers often had to pay his debts. Then Sarah and Daniel's luck seemed to change. He got a job as the county jailer, and the family, as was common back then, lived in the jailhouse, where Sarah did the cooking and cleaning. She and Daniel also cleaned the courthouse, another source of income. But then misfortune struck, and in 1816 Daniel died of cholera. By 1819, when Thomas came to town, Sarah seemed to be prospering—she owned a cabin filled with good furniture, and one of her daughters was attending a private school. Tom had hit pay dirt. The story of their brief courtship was told to a correspondent for the *Atlantic* by a physician in Jasper, Arkansas—a son of one of Lincoln's nieces who had been raised in Tom and Nancy's home:

> Thomas Lincoln made a short trip to Kentucky, and while there married a widow, a Mrs. Johnston. "Mother said she was his old sweetheart, before he ever saw Nancy Hanks," related the doctor. "When he went back, I guess he had her in view. When he got there, she was washing in the yard. He went along just like he was walking by and leant up against the fence and talked to her. He proposed marriage, and she said, 'I owe too much.' 'How

much?' Uncle Tom asked her, and she replied, 'Two dollars and a half.' Uncle Tom volunteered, 'If that's all, I'll pay that'; and the match was made up right there. I've heard mother laughing about that many a time." (Arthur E. Morgan, "New Light on Lincoln's Boyhood")

While Mrs. Johnston was lacking in ready money, yet according to the doctor, "She was right good for property. She had right smart." And Uncle Tom brought back not only a wife, but a wagonload of her furniture.

Sarah had three young children, so besides organizing the Lincolns, she brought new life into the isolated family. A copy of the marriage bond between Thomas and Sarah is at the Hardin County Public Library in Elizabethtown. A replica of the cabin where Sarah Bush Johnston and her three children were living when Thomas came courting is located at Freeman Lake Park. It's a pretty scene, but, I warn you, after a while all these log cabins begin to look the same—there seems to have been only one basic model with occasional upgrades, as realtors today would call them, such as a loft or second floor, or maybe even a passageway where a horse and wagon could be stowed between the kitchen area and the bedrooms. Having a horse or two nearly inside probably didn't make much difference when it came to odors. After all, those cabins brimmed with unbathed people, chamber pots, and dirty clothes. Sarah, though, was not the average woman, and history says she cleaned up Thomas's cabin and his kids. She was that kind of person.

Other Traces of Lincoln

In downtown Elizabethtown, a cabinet made by Thomas Lincoln is on display at the Brown-Pusey House. The home was built in 1825 and is considered one of the best examples of rural Federal architecture in the town. It also boasts an extensive and well-respected research library and a lovely garden.

There are other Lincoln associations with the Brown-Pusey House as well, some tangential, but all connecting dots between the Civil War, the Lincoln family, and the people and places who

A cabinet made by Thomas Lincoln, a skilled carpenter, is on display at the Brown-Pusey House, in Elizabethtown. *Photo courtesy of Wikimedia*

defined the times. Confederate General John Hunt Morgan, whose life intersected with Thomas's brother Josiah Lincoln's, dined there several times. Morgan—a dashing and impetuous soldier known for his fondness for good wine, good food, pretty women, and a comfortable bed (not for him the hardships of a soldier's life)—hailed from Lexington, and his family home, now a house museum, is within walking distance of Mary Todd Lincoln's home, also a museum, and the law offices of Henry Clay, at one time a great hero to Lincoln. General George Custer and his wife would move into the Brown-Pusey Home much later, after Custer was sent to help control the rise of the Ku Klux Klan. There's no connection to Lincoln in the case of Custer, but it is an interesting factoid.

Sisters-in-Law from Hell

The Elizabethtown Historic Driving Tour includes many late-eighteenth-century sites and further Lincoln connections.

For example, the McKinney-Helm House, circa 1820, at 218 West Poplar Street, was at one time owned by Emilie Todd Helm, half-sister of Mary Todd Lincoln and widow of Confederate general Ben Hardin Helm. Emilie was pretty, pert, and seemingly spoiled, with a bio that reads like that of Scarlett O'Hara in *Gone with the Wind*. Like many of Mary's half-siblings, the children of Mary's father and her despised stepmother, Emilie was a true, die-hard Confederate. Her husband declined a job as an army paymaster when President Lincoln offered it to him and instead joined the Confederate Army. That didn't work out too well for him—he was only thirty-two when he died in the awful Battle of Chickamauga in 1863. His death was an emotional blow for both Mary and Abe. In December of that year, Emilie and her daughter came to stay for a time at the White House. Lincoln was criticized for having her there and reportedly defended his decision by saying, "Mrs. Lincoln and I will allow anyone we choose to visit us in the White House."

In her diary Emilie wrote,

> Mr. Lincoln in the intimate talks we had was very much affected over the misfortunes of our family; and of my husband he said, "You know, Little Sister, I tried to have Ben come with me. I hope you do not feel any bitterness or that I am in any way to blame for all this sorrow."
>
> I answered it was "the fortune of war" and that while my husband loved him and had been deeply grateful to him for his generous offer to make him an officer in the Federal Army, he had to follow his conscience and that for weal or woe he felt he must side with his own people. Mr. Lincoln put his arms around me and we both wept. (Katherine Helm, *The True Story of Mary, Wife of Lincoln*, 233)

But the Lincoln's kindness toward Emilie started wearing thin. In the summer of 1864, Lincoln had her brought to the White House because she refused, when detained at Fort Monroe in Virginia, to vow loyalty to the Union.

In a diary entry about this forced visit, Emilie wrote,

Mr. Lincoln and my sister met me with the warmest affection, we were all too grief-stricken at first for speech. I have lost my husband, they have lost their fine little son Willie. Mary and I have lost three brothers in the Confederate service. We could only embrace each other in silence and tears. Our tears gathered silently and fell unheeded as with choking voices we tried to talk of immaterial things. (Helm, *The True Story*, 221–22)

Emilie was quite bold about her Confederate loyalties, especially given she was staying at the White House over many people's objections, some of whom called her "The Rebel." Despite their shared grief, she fought with Mary over who the real president of the country was. Mary, of course, said it was her husband. Emilie said no, it was Jefferson Davis.

Emilie's tongue was tart and her manner arrogant. When a US senator said to her, "We have whipped the rebels at Chattanooga, and I hear the scoundrels ran like scared rabbits," she was quick with her reply. "It was the example you set them at Bull Run and Manassas."

She did finally take an oath of allegiance but continued to support Confederate causes. In August 1864, Lincoln had finally had enough and wrote General Stephen G. Burbridge stating that he was not giving Emilie any protection against prosecution for her actions: "If the paper given her by me can be construed to give her protection for such words so, it is hereby revoked *pro tanto*. Deal with her for current conduct, just as you would any other" (Roy P. Basler, *Collected Works of Abraham Lincoln*, 485).

Do you think that stopped Emilie from asking for favors? If you said yes, you need to go rent a copy of *Gone with the Wind*. Like Scarlet O'Hara, Emilie seems to have had an immense sense of entitlement. We don't know if she stamped her feet like Scarlet did, but in November she asked for another pass to sell her cotton, writing to Lincoln in a somewhat waspish tone, "I have been a quiet citizen and request only the right which humanity and justice always gives to widows and orphans. I also would remind you that your minié bullets have made us what we are" (Ruth Painter Randall, *Mary Todd Lincoln*) She seemed to be missing the point that the Union had widows and orphans made so by Confederate bullets. And besides, who had started the damn war?

Emilie never remarried, wearing widow's weeds for the remainder of her life. She died at age ninety-three and is buried in the Lexington Cemetery, along with so many of Mary Todd's family and friends and those who intersected with the Lincolns, including John Hunt Morgan.

Martha Todd White, another of Mary Lincoln's half-sisters, was also a gung-ho supporter of the Confederacy. Because of her family connection she received a pass to come north, but despite her requests for an invitation to the White House, her Confederate sympathies were such that she was denied. Lincoln finally threatened that if she didn't leave DC immediately she'd be confined to the Old Capitol Prison. She took the hint and left, but she returned later wanting a permit to export cotton to the north, a move that would help bolster the Confederate economy as well as her own pocketbook. Lincoln was not about to let happen.

Bright, pretty, and popular, Mary smuggled "almost her weight in quinine" through the lines for sick Southern soldiers. The result was less quinine for sick Union men. It's said she bragged about how she outwitted her "brother Lincoln."

Relatives, right? What are you going to do?

HARRODSBURG, KENTUCKY

Pleasant Hill: The Original Peaceniks

Northeast of Elizabethtown are remnants of Shaker communities that were thriving in Lincoln's time. Lincoln would have been well aware of the Shakers, at that time a dominant force offering an appealing ideal of communal living. Ahead of their time in many ways, members of United Society of Believers in Christ's Second Appearance, called Shakers because of their ecstatic movements during prayer, abolished slavery among their

A horse and wagon travels along a road lined with buildings dating back to the early 1800s. Shaker Village of Pleasant Hill is America's largest restored Shaker village. *Photo courtesy of Jane Simon Ammeson*

own and bought slaves for the purpose of freeing them. In 1817, they granted women equal rights—a century or more before all women in the United States would be allowed to vote. They also, rather amazingly, let women hold positions of power in their community. Their industriousness brought them prosperity.

Though Lincoln never visited either of the Shaker villages in Kentucky, the Shakers' abolitionist views were in sync with his own and a number of Shaker communities are located near sites where Lincoln lived. Dating back to the early 1800s, Shaker Village of Pleasant Hill just outside of Harrodsburg was once the third largest Shaker community in the United States and it is now one of only a few Shaker settlements with buildings still standing. And though the Shakers who lived here and in South Union Shaker Village in Auburn, Kentucky, are gone, historic preservationists are dedicated to retaining the charm of these historic sites by immaculately restoring the buildings

The Kentucky River was a source of livelihood for the Shakers. The same landing used by the Shakers is now the launching point of the *Dixie Belle*, Shaker Village's paddlewheeler, and is also one of the few public access points to the beautiful Kentucky River Palisades. *Photo courtesy of Jane Simon Ammeson*

and showcasing how life was lived in one of the most successful utopian communities in American history.

Pleasant Hill, approximately eighty miles from Elizabethtown via Martha Layne Collins Blue Grass Parkway East to US 127 South, is the only national historic landmark where visitors can spend the night in the same rooms Shakers lived and worked in. The winding roads in the area lead through small, quaint, charming towns. A few miles from the entrance to Pleasant Hill a narrow road winds down a steep hillside to the dock of the *Dixie Belle* riverboat, where up to 115 visitors can take a one-hour cruise through the soaring palisades of this largely undeveloped section of the Kentucky River. The tour guide explains how important transportation was for the community, which sold its goods as far south as New Orleans.

A landmark destination located in Harrodsburg, the three-thousand-acre Shaker Village of Pleasant Hill was home to the third largest Shaker population in the United States. The Shakers were among the earliest abolitionists and also believed in equal rights for women.
Photo courtesy of Jane Simon Ammeson

Preserving the uniqueness of the Shakers' heritage is part of the mission of both South Union Shaker Village and Pleasant Hill. In 1840 around six thousand Shakers lived in nineteen communal villages in New England, Indiana, Ohio, and Kentucky. Only one remains today, its membership down to two. But the ideals of pacifism, communal living, taking care of each other, and focusing on spirituality rather than worldly goods still seem worthy goals.

On the Kentucky River, Shaker Hill of Pleasant Village is near where the Civil War Battle of Perryville took place, and many of the wounded were brought there for care. "The Shakers took in anyone, whether they were Union or Confederate, who needed tending," says Aaron Genton, collections manager at

Thomas Lincoln and Nancy Hanks were married in a log cabin belonging to Richard Berry in the small hamlet of Beachland near Springfield on June 12, 1806. That cabin is now protected from the elements by a brick museum at the Lincoln Marriage Temple in Harrodsburg. *Photo courtesy of Jane Simon Ammeson*

Pleasant Hill, which is located just outside of Harrodsburg, the oldest city in Kentucky. "But they were certainly in support of the Union and Lincoln's policies."

The Lincoln Marriage Temple

The Lincoln Marriage Temple in Harrodsburg, a stop on Kentucky's Lincoln Heritage Trail, is an odd-sounding name (maybe a little too Las Vegas–like?), but the intent to honor the Lincolns is real. The red brick building encasing the log cabin where Tom and Nancy got married is part of the Old Fort Harrod State Park in downtown Harrodsburg. Also part of the park are the historic Mansion Museum, the George Rogers Clark Federal Monument, and the oldest cemetery west of the Alleghenies.

Kentucky Owl

Bourbon and Lincoln history again cross paths in Harrodsburg. The stately Beaumont Inn was built in 1825 and functioned as a school for girls before being bought by the Dedman family in 1917, who have operated it as an inn ever since. The James Beard Award–winning dining room is just one part of what makes this a great stop for anyone visiting Harrodsburg. Dixon Dedman, who owns the inn along with his parents, is also famed for his bourbon tastings and his revival of the bourbon his great-great-grandfather used to make before Prohibition shut him down.

Dedman is the creator of Kentucky Owl distillery, where he makes small batches of his limited-release and top-rated Kentucky Owl rye whiskey. "It's an 11-year-old Kentucky Straight Rye Whiskey and it's exactly what a Rye Whiskey should be," Dixon writes on Kentucky Owl's Facebook page about his most recent batch. "I put this blend together and bottled it at 110.6 proof. It's a full-flavored rye perfect for the coming fall weather."

Barrel aging can produce bourbons with a high proof, but before they're bottled, they're watered down to around 80 proof.

Dixon wasn't about to do that to Kentucky Owl. "It's full fla-vored," he said about this batch of Kentucky Owl, and it sure was. "You can't hide anything in barrel proofed whiskeys."

SHELBYVILLE, KENTUCKY

The Boones and Painted Stone Station

Because the Boones and the Lincolns were interconnected, I thought I'd segue into a little Boone family history here. Squire Boone, the brother of the more famous Daniel, was also an ex-plorer and woodsman and famed in his day for his exploits in opening up Indiana and Kentucky to settlers. Back then both states were wild, dangerous, and unexplored. Of the first eight white men to enter Kentucky, Squire and Daniel were the only two to come out alive—and it was Squire who rescued Daniel. The two were said to be such excellent trackers that they could agree to meet at a certain time on a certain day and each take a separate route into the wilderness—returning at the exact time and place they'd agreed on. No GPS needed for these guys.

Ten years younger than Daniel but filled with the same wan-derlust, Squire Boone established Painted Stone Station in 1780, the first settlement in Shelby County, about fifteen miles from the Old Stone Inn. It was the only station between Harrodsburg and what is now Louisville. The nearest station at the time was Linn's, twenty-one miles distant, which even on a fast horse would take two hours or more to reach. So even if someone man-aged to escape under siege, help couldn't be expected to arrive for at least four or five hours. A battle could very well be finished by then. At its peak, one hundred people lived at Painted Stone Station; unfortunately, it didn't work out well for them.

Painted Stone Is Attacked: The Long Run Massacre

In April of 1781, Boone's Station came under attack and the alarm was sounded, Squire Boone, in his shirttails, and about a dozen other men seized their guns and ran to its defense, where they were waylaid by about twenty Indians. Boone, covering the retreat of his comrades, received two gunshot wounds—one breaking his right arm just below the elbow, and the other hitting him in his right side. Despite his serious injuries he was still able to make it back inside the stockade.

The leader of the attack was Simon Girty, a notorious renegade who had been captured by the Seneca Indians in his youth and adopted into the tribe. In 1778, after going over to the British, he had served as scout and interpreter. He would be present when Colonel William Crawford was tortured and burned at the stake in 1782 in retaliation for the brutal massacre of ninety-six peaceful Christian Indian men, women, and children who had been slaughtered by Pennsylvanian militiamen, although Colonel Crawford had not been among them.

Girty would later boast that he had made Squire Boone's white shirt fly with his shots. For a while there was concern Boone wouldn't survive, but he recovered in about three months. Though his arm healed, it was about an inch and a half shorter than it had been, and a long while after the battle, splinters of bone would work their way out of his skin.

That wasn't the end of it. Learning they were going to be attacked again that September, some of the settlers at Painted Stone Station (named after a stone Squire had decorated to mark the place) fled for a safer station, and some were killed before they made it. Squire Boone and his family, along with one other family, remained at the station and were rescued a few days later. Squire returned two years later to find Painted Stone Station had been burned to the ground. He stayed to rebuild it, and even added a gristmill.

Though unknown to many Americans, the story of Painted Stone Station is very well known in Shelby County. For over twenty years, there's been an annual reenactment of the events known as the Long Run Massacre and Floyd's Defeat, held the second full weekend in September at Red Orchard Park in

Autumn Nethery, distiller and co-owner of Jeptha Creed distillery, stands in front of some of their products. Jeptha Creed is distilled from grain grown on Jeptha Knob, named by Daniel and Squire Boone. *Photo courtesy of Jane Simon Ammeson*

Shelbyville, which is just a few miles from the Old Stone Inn and Captain Abraham Lincoln's gravesite.

Like Tom Lincoln, Squire too had land disputes (Kentucky was notorious for that) and also, according to contemporary accounts, liked to gamble too much, which led to his losing much of his land and money.

Jeptha Creed Distillery

As you know, I always seem to have bourbon on my mind, so I'll mention that the recently opened Jeptha Creed Distillery in Shelbyville is on land near where Painted Rock most likely stood. Jeptha Creed is owned by the Nethery family, and the moonshine, vodka, and bourbon they distill is made from the open-pollinated, non-GMO, heirloom Bloody Butcher corn they've been growing since 1845 on their Jeptha Knob farm, located about six miles from the distillery. And here's the tie-in with Daniel and Squire: the Boone brothers are the ones who named the land back in the late 1700s after the biblical warrior and judge Jephthah. Isn't that a good enough reason to stop by for a taste?

PIONEER STOCK: THE BOONES

We'd be remiss not to share some more about the Boone family, as their history reflects the times they lived in, giving us another window into the life of early pioneer families, including the Lincolns. George Boone, who was born about 1670 at his old family home eight miles from Exeter, England, arrived with his wife, Mary, and the couple's eleven children (nine sons and two daughters) in Philadelphia on October 10, 1717. Purchasing a tract of land in what is now Berks County, Pennsylvania, Boone named it Exeter after his hometown in England. One of George and Mary's sons, Squire, married Sarah Morgan on July 23, 1720. They also had eleven children, seven boys and four girls. Their oldest boy, James, was killed by Indians.

Sarah and Squire's son Daniel was born October 22, 1734. He was described as having a restless pioneer spirit; a chronicler writes that Daniel "early began his adventurous travels, although he had a good education for the times, and was a skilled land surveyor" (State Historical Society of Missouri, "Lincoln, Hanks and Boone Families"). Daniel married Rebecca Bryant on August 14, 1756, when he was twenty and she was seventeen, after a three-year courtship. During a twenty-nine-year period, Rebecca had six sons and four daughters, which is pretty remarkable in itself, and even more so considering Daniel was often away on long trips. Not only did they have their own large brood, Daniel and Rebecca also took in a large number of children who had been orphaned (a very common occurrence back then). Right before the birth of Rebecca's ninth child, she welcomed her widowed uncle's six children, ranging in age from six to sixteen. Described as tall and very pretty, Rebecca was also the midwife and the family healer for the communities she lived in, as well as a leather tanner, sharpshooter, and linen maker. How she had time for all this, we don't know. All I can say is, "Go, Rebecca, go."

To make it more complicated—and isn't that just typical of life—it's said that on one of Daniel's many long expeditions (this one lasted two years), Rebecca, believing he was dead, dallied with Daniel's brother Edward and became pregnant. Though that made things a little dicey between the two brothers, Daniel accepted his brother's daughter, who was named Jemima, as his own. We don't know if Jemima knew that her father was really her uncle and her uncle her father. Even more soap opera–ish, Edward was married to Rebecca's sister Martha, and the couple had six children. Poor Neddy, as he was called, was said to be a kindly and affable guy who stayed behind when Daniel and the others went exploring to take care of community matters.

Neddy came to an unfortunate end when on a hunting trip with his brother. The two men were returning from a trip to the Blue Licks when they stopped along a stream in Bourbon County near Paris. There Edward rested underneath a buckeye tree, cracking nuts and watching the horses as they drank. Daniel, who was in the woods hunting game, heard shots being fired by Indians and hid until they left. Stories diverge here. Some say Daniel returned to find Edward riddled with seven musket balls. Another version says he ran on foot to Boone Station, where he and his brother and about fifteen other families were living. The following morning, Daniel and a group of men went in search of the Indians but they were gone. Finding Edward's body, they buried him where he died, near the old buckeye tree. The creek where Edward met his end was named Boone Creek in his honor.

By 1827, rain and erosion had exposed Edward's bones, and he was reinterred about a mile away. When his gravesite fell into disrepair, it was restored, and the Edward Boone Death Site was designated a Kentucky Landmark by the Kentucky Heritage

Council. Later, a Kentucky Historical Highway Marker was established at KY Highway 537 and See Road, about a mile east of Little Rock.

Daniel and Rebecca spent the last years of their fifty-eight years of marriage (imagine that) living with Jemima and Flanders Callaway, their son-in-law. Rebecca died in 1813 at age seventy-five; Daniel lived until the age of eighty-five, dying in 1820. They are now buried in Frankfort Cemetery in Frankfort, Kentucky.

The Boones and Callaways had been friends for many years, going back to when Jemima Boone and Fanny and Betsey Callaway, fourteen-year-old girls who lived at Boonesborough, Kentucky, were captured while canoeing on the Kentucky River by a war party of three Shawnee men and two Cherokee men, led by the Cherokee Hanging Maw. Native American tribes like the Shawnee frequently attacked Kentucky settlements in attempts to drive out the people they saw as stealing their land. The attacks became so violent that by late spring of 1776, fewer than two hundred settlers remained, and those who did mostly lived in the fortified stations at Boonesborough, Harrodsburg, and Logan's Station.

Fanny and Betsey were the daughters of Colonel Richard Callaway, who, along with his son Flanders, joined Daniel Boone in a search party. The Indians were taking the girls north toward their towns, and as they moved, the girls tried to leave a trail to be followed. Although their captors made them stop, the search party was still able to sneak up on them. As a shot rang out, injuring one of the Indians, Jemima supposedly shouted, "That's Daddy's gun." What can I say? It's a good daughter who knows the sound of her father's gun.

When asked by their rescuers if they were okay, Jemima replied, like a true Boone, that the Indians had been kind to them, "as much so as they well could have been, or their circumstances permitted."

It isn't known if the rescue added to their romance, but the three girls each married one of the rescuers. A month after their escape, Elizabeth Callaway married Samuel Henderson. The following year, Jemima married Flanders Callaway, and Fanny Callaway married Colonel John Holder. The story of the kidnapping and rescue was the basis for the novel and the movie *The Last of the Mohicans*.

In a sad aside, Jemima and Flanders's oldest son, James Callaway, would be shot and killed by Indians. Callaway County in Missouri is named after him, and a war memorial located in Fulton, Missouri, was erected in his honor. Two of Jemima's brothers, James and Israel, were also killed by Indians. John Stewart, Jemima's uncle and the husband of Daniel's sister Hannah, died the same way.

PLACES TO VISIT

Abraham Lincoln Birthplace National Historical Park
2995 Lincoln Farm Road
Hodgenville, KY
(270) 358-3137; nps.gov/abli/index.htm

Abraham Lincoln's Boyhood Home at Knob Creek
7120 Bardstown Road
Hodgenville, KY
(270) 358-3137; nps.gov/abli/planyourvisit/boyhood-home.htm

Beaumont Inn
638 Beaumont Inn Drive
Harrodsburg, KY
(859) 734-3381; beaumontinn.com

Boone Station Historical Site
240 Gentry Road
Athens, KY
(859) 263-1073

Boundary Oak Distillery
2000 Boundary Oak Drive
Radcliff, KY
(270) 351-2013; BoundaryOakDistillery.com

Brown-Pusey House
128 North Main Street
Elizabethtown, KY
(270) 765-2515; brownpuseyhouse.org

Captain Abraham Lincoln's Gravesite
Long Run Cemetery
Old Stage Coach Road
Eastwood
Jefferson County, KY

Edward Boone Death Site
KY Highway 537 and See Road, about a mile east of Little Rock
Eleanor Hamilton's Old Stone Inn
6905 Shelbyville Road
Simpsonville, KY
(502) 722-8200; eholdstoneinn.com

Fort Boonesborough State Park
4375 Boonesboro Road
Richmond, KY
(859) 527-3131; parks.ky.gov/parks/recreationparks
/fort-boonesborough

Frankfort Cemetery
East Main Street
Frankfort, KY

Fort Knox Saber & Quill
1118 Chaffee Avenue
Fort Knox, KY
(859) 734-3314; knox.armymwr.com/programs/saber-quill

Hardin County History Museum
201 West Dixie Avenue
Elizabethtown, KY
(270) 763-8339; kentuckytourism.com/
hardin-county-history-museum/184

Hardin County Public Library
100 Jim Owen Drive
Elizabethtown, KY
(270) 769-6337; hcpl.info

Jeptha Creed
500 Gordon Lane
Shelbyville, KY
(502) 487-5007; jepthacreed.com

Kentucky's Lincoln Museum
66 Lincoln Square
Hodgenville, KY
(270) 358-3163; incolnmuseum-ky.org/Index.html

Lincoln and Civil War Legacy Trail
https://www.enjoyillinois.com/explore/listing/
lincoln-and-civil-war-legacy-trail

Lincoln Homestead State Park
KY 258
Springfield, KY
(859) 336-7461; parks.ky.gov/parks/recreationparks
/lincoln-homestead/

The Lincoln Marriage Temple
Old Fort Harrod State Park
100 South College Street
Harrodsburg, KY
(859) 734-3314; parks.ky.gov/parks/recreationparks
/fort-harrod

Mordecai Lincoln House at Lincoln Homestead State Park
KY 258
Springfield, KY
(859) 336-7461; parks.ky.gov/parks/recreationparks
/lincoln-homestead

Old Fort Harrod State Park
100 South College Street
Harrodsburg, KY
(859) 734-3314; parks.ky.gov/parks/recreationparks
/fort-harrod

Painted Stone Settlement
The Annual reenactment is held at Red Orchard Park:
709 Red Orchard Park
Shelbyville, KY
info@paintedstonesettler.org; paintedstonesettlers.org

Sarah Johnston Lincoln Cabin
Blue Heron Way
Freeman Lake Park
Elizabethtown, KY 42701
(270) 769-3916

Shaker Village of Pleasant Hill
3501 Lexington Road
Harrodsburg, KY 40330
(859) 734-5411

Abraham Lincoln was born in a meager, one-room cabin about 20 miles south of Bardstown in Hodgenville, KY.

It had a dirt floor, one window, and a stick-clay chimney. Lincoln's father, Tom, had paid $200 for the cabin and 300 acres of discouraging land. It wasn't much, but it was a home and a chance for a better life.

After four years of fighting mosquitos, heat and hardscrabble land, the Lincolns had to pack up and leave. There was a defect in the title. A trial was held at the Courthouse in Bardstown around 1812. The family stayed here at the Tavern. Abraham was quoted as being clad in a "one-piece long linsey shirt."

Sign in front of the Lincoln Room
at the Old Talbott Tavern,
Bardstown, Kentucky.

2

BARDSTOWN AND BOURBON

OLD TALBOTT TAVERN

"Abraham Lincoln was about five years old when he stayed here," says Deanna Kelley, whose husband's family has owned the inn for decades. "It's kind of crazy to think that he used to be here, in this very building." The tavern first opened in 1779. At that time, a large number of taverns and inns lined the rudimentary roads crisscrossing America. In the Colonial and Early American eras, restaurants as we know them didn't really exist outside of major cities such as New York and Philadelphia, and even there they were rare. Instead, inns, stagecoach stops, and taverns made up the perfect trifecta for travelers: beds, edibles, and strong spirits. Now very few of these establishments remain. The Old Talbott Tavern is considered one of the oldest taverns in continuous operation in the United States and the oldest stage-coach stop west of the Allegheny Mountains.

Lincoln wasn't the only famous personage to stay at the Old Talbott Tavern. Others included Daniel Boone (and probably

Located in downtown Bardstown, the Old Talbott Tavern first opened in 1779. The room here looks much like it would have when the Lincoln family stayed there before moving to Indiana—albeit there's now electricity and other comforts of the twenty-first century.
Photo courtesy of Jane Simon Ammeson

his brother Squire, who also owned a lot of land in Kentucky, lost it, and had to head north to Indiana) and General George Rogers Clark, whose younger brother, William Clark, led the famed Lewis and Clark expedition. George himself helped win the day during the Revolutionary War with a sneak attack on the British culminating in a victory at the Battle of Vincennes. General George Patton was a guest, as was Stephen Foster, who wrote many songs, including "Beautiful Dreamer," "Camptown Races," and "Old Folks at Home." Foster also often stayed at Federal Hill, the Rowan Home built in Bardstown in 1818, said to be the inspiration for probably his most famous song, "My

Old Kentucky Home." The Rowan Home is well worth the visit, and not only for its elegant beauty—where else will docents suddenly burst into song? Other guests at the Old Talbott Tavern included Jesse James, who got drunk there and shot at imaginary butterflies. (It happens, okay?) The bullet holes went through murals painted by exiled king Louis Philippe of France. It was that kind of place, though I assure you it's much calmer nowadays.

The Dry Stone Masonry Institute of America describes the tavern as a "uniquely well-crafted early American stone building and an extremely rare example of Flemish bond stonework . . . illustrating the excellent craftsmanship of the settlement period." To the visitor, the tavern, with its thick walls, original timbered ceiling, built-in wood cabinets, and wide doorways, has a centuries-old charm and feel despite such updates as electricity and running water. That feel of times long gone by is particularly poignant when I enter early one morning and appear to be the only one in the dining area. As I stand in this room with its large fireplaces original to the building, looking out the deep inset casement windows with their glass gone wavy from the settling of centuries in the half-light of morning before the lights have been switched on, I wonder what would happen if I turned around quickly. Would I get a glimpse of a young Lincoln watching food being cooked over a roaring fire? Or, with worse luck, Jesse James shooting off his gun?

The original fare, some of which still graces the menu, would have provided ample sustenance for travelers. Diners today can fill up on such southern traditions as fried chicken, biscuits, and mashed potatoes. In Lincoln's time there would also have been burgoo, a true Kentucky classic—a type of thick stew with a variety of meats (depending on what the hunters brought home that day, which could have been squirrel, rabbit, fat hens, pigeon, and even blackbird) and vegetables (depending on what was in the garden). The dish is said to have originated with Gustave Jaubert, a French chef who lived in Lexington. Jaubert served his burgoo to General John Hunt Morgan and his Confederate

Raiders and was then hired by Buffalo Trace Distillery in Frankfort to cook for their workers. Two of Jaubert's huge iron burgoo kettles are on display at the distillery. In another connection to Lincoln, in 1862, Confederate soldiers took over the Old Talbott Tavern for two weeks to use as a staging area for the Battle of Perryville, a divisive win for Union troops.

"The doors are wide like that because women had to get through them with their hoop skirts," Old Tablott owner Deanna Kelley explains. Women in wide skirts (always a fire hazard) also cooked over the two large fireplaces that flank the sides of the door leading into a second dining area. "They would have served a lot of game in those days," says Kelley when I ask what the Lincoln family would have eaten back then. "It would be what might have been shot that day. We don't have game on the menu anymore; it's gotten too hard to get." In other words, don't expect to find a menu of fried squirrel, partridge, venison, or—yikes!—raccoon, which Lincoln was said to favor. Dishes are cooked in the kitchen now, not over the open fire. In Lincoln's day, chicken was fried in large cast-iron skillets, and Kelley says they fry their chicken the same way. But, no, she tells me, they're not the same skillets.

Kentucky Bourbon

Lincoln would have been too young to partake of Bardstown's rich bourbon history, but surely his father, Thomas, bellied up to the bar, particularly during the legal dispute over his farmland. "William Heavenhill, who owned the property where Heaven Hill Distillery is located, frequented the tavern," says Kelley. Embroiled in a lawsuit, the Lincolns would have needed a place to stay while the court proceedings took place, and the tavern is just across the street from the Nelson County Courthouse.

Bardstown, located in the rolling hills of Kentucky's Bluegrass region, is home to a plethora of small distilleries where bourbon was made both for private use and to sell, and the town is now a major stop on the Kentucky Bourbon Trail. The spirits' roots date back the mid- to late 1700s. That's when many

Scotch-Irish and southerners from Appalachia who knew how to distill spirits settled here, some in part escaping the whiskey tax imposed by George Washington in 1791, which ultimately led to the Whiskey Rebellion.

"Bourbon is a legacy of blue grass and Kentucky limestone," says Carol Peachee, a professional photographer and author of *Straight Bourbon: Distilling the Industry's Heritage*. Peachee notes that the terroir of Central Kentucky, where a layer of limestone filters the iron from the water, creates excellent conditions for bourbon making.

After a long day in court, upon returning to the tavern, Tom Lincoln might have sipped—and maybe even gulped, given how dire the Lincoln's situation was—local bourbons. The offerings at the inn might have included spirits distilled by Jacob Beam (originally Boehm), who in 1795 sold his first barrel of "Old Jake Beam Sour Mash" made at his Old Tub Distillery. His company, still in business today, is, of course, Jim Beam.

Tom Lincoln also might have sipped the whiskey made by Elijah Pepper, who in 1812 started a distillery west of Lexington; some of that distillery's old stone buildings make up what is now the Woodford Reserve in Versailles. But those wouldn't have been his only choices. Daniel Weller opened his distillery, now W. L. Weller Bourbon, in 1794. Basil Hayden bottled his Old Grand-Dad in 1785. In approximately 1789, Elijah Craig, a preacher, opened a distillery in Bardstown as well.

Tom almost certainly imbibed the bourbon made by Wattie Boone, a relative of Daniel Boone, who built the first distillery on Knob Creek around 1780, called Boone Distillery. Tom Lincoln worked there in the early to mid-1810s, around the time the Lincolns moved from Sinking Spring Farm to Knob Creek Farm.

It could be whiskey was an issue for Tom. It's said that the reason he was forced to sell the family farm in 1816 for twenty dollars and four hundred gallons of whiskey was partly due to his own overconsumption. But that's another part of the family history that is very much contested. "He had taken one whole month's rent on the farm in advance in pints of whiskey," says Bill Samuels, chairman emeritus of Maker's Mark Distillery. "It's there in the records." Samuels is an inductee into the Kentucky Bourbon Hall of Fame, whose great-great-great-great-grandfather operated a still in Pennsylvania in 1779 and moved to Kentucky in 1780. Samuels has another good reason to be in on the family dirt: his wife is a descendent of Wattie Boone. It's obviously a bourbon kind of family.

If Tom Lincoln had a liquor problem—his great-uncle Tom supposedly lost his profitable distilling business because he sampled too much of his own product—that might be the reason why his son Abe hardly drank at all, despite the fact that it was a hard-drinking time in our nation's history. Water, after

Woodford Reserve, outside of Bardstown, is another stop on the Kentucky Bourbon Trail and includes old stone buildings from Lincoln's time. *Photo courtesy of Kentuckytourism.com*

LINCOLN ROAD TRIP

Heaven Hill Bourbon Heritage Center in Bardstown is a good place to learn about the area's bourbon history. *Photo courtesy of Kentuckytourism.com*

all, wasn't necessarily safe to drink. Liquor could also be used in lieu of money. Lincoln's father took several barrels with him to Indiana to trade for farmland.

I'm not encouraging you to visit and sample at all these distilleries, but if you're interested, a good starting place is the Heaven Hill Bourbon Heritage Center in Bardstown. From there, it's fifteen miles southeast to Maker's Mark Distillery in Loretto. Or you can go northwest to Clermont to visit the Jim Beam American Stillhouse. Woodford Reserve Distillery lies fifty-five miles northeast of Bardstown. The website of the Kentucky Bourbon Trail Experience features a downloadable map showing the mileage between these distilleries and others in the state.

All this bourbon history is preserved and presented at the Oscar Getz Museum of Whiskey History located in historic Spalding Hall in Bardstown, within walking distance of the Old Talbott Tavern. Built around 1826, Spalding Hall was first a seminary and then a hospital for both Union and Confederate troops during the Civil War, so it seems fitting that this grand old building now also houses the Civil War Museum. At the Oscar Getz Museum, visitors can follow the history of spirits from the Whiskey Rebellion to the present day. There's also a small section about Lincoln with some artifacts, including a diorama of his tavern and store in Illinois and a copy of his liquor license from there.

Mary and Elizabeth Owens and the Sisters of Charity of Nazareth Academy

Bardstown had the first Catholic cathedral west of the Allegheny Mountains, so the Catholic presence is strong there and would play an important role in the life of Mary Owens, the woman who almost married Abraham Lincoln.

On April 13, 1816, Mary Owens and her sister, Elizabeth, known as Betsy, from Green County, Kentucky, enrolled in the Sisters of Charity of Nazareth Academy located just outside of Bardstown, a little over three miles going north on Bardstown Road. Mary, who was called Polly at school, was eight and Betsy, ten. Though the school was predominantly Catholic, the Owens sisters were Protestant. Their parents must have thought an education was important, as tuition cost $100—approximately $1,868.46 in today's money. The total for both girls would come close to $4000 per year, not an insignificant sum to educate girls who would, after all, only go on to marry and have babies.

The academy wasn't just a finishing school for wealthy girls either—one that offered the type of fluff thought necessary for landing a rich husband. Its curriculum was challenging. "We offered astronomy, hard sciences, mathematics, and languages," says Kathy Hertel-Baker, director of archives at the Sisters of Charity of Nazareth Archival Center. According to Hertel-Baker, five nieces of Jefferson Davis, the president of the Confederacy, also attended the academy, which opened in 1814. Now, though the academy is closed, the campus grounds are an inviting place to wander and meditate. The sisters take such good care of their documents that Mary's and Betsy's handwritten enrollment cards, some two centuries old, are still on file.

The fact that Mary and Betsy would play a part in Lincoln's life—Betsy almost arranged a marriage between Mary and Lincoln— and their association with the academy are often thought to be the reasons why Lincoln would issue special orders for it to be protected during the Civil War. Today a beautiful and charming town, Bardstown was much more chaotic as the Civil War was coming to a close. Back then, Bardstown went back and forth between occupation by Union and Confederate troops, and the sisters and their supporters often feared for their safety.

As I sit in the second-floor Archival Center, Hertel-Baker goes to their cold storage archives and brings back a handwritten note enclosed in a protective sheath. I am looking at words that Abraham Lincoln wrote just months before he was murdered. They show how even at an exceptionally tumultuous time in our nation's history, when the stresses and demands upon him must have been almost overwhelming, Lincoln took the time to ensure the safety of the academy.

> Let no depredation be committed upon the property or possession of the "Sisters of Charity" at Nazareth Academy near Bardstown, Ky.
> January 17, 1865
> A. Lincoln.

This order, preserved by the sisters, has a counterpart explaining its origin.

> Senate Chamber, Washington,
> Jan. 17, 1865
> Miss Columba Carroll,
> Mother Superior of Nazareth.
> Bardstown, KY.,
> I received your letter of the 9th Jan. two days ago. I called on the President this morning and presented your case for his

consideration. He promptly gave me a safe-guard which I enclose herewith; it will protect you from further depredations. It affords me pleasure to serve you in this matter. If I can serve you further, command me.

Respectfully,

L. W. Powell.

The Hon. James Guthrie of Kentucky appealed to Lincoln for a further guarantee of the academy's safety, and the president then issued an order of military significance declaring that "any violation thereof would incur his serious displeasure."

Lawyer Lincoln and Mary Owens

In 1822, Betsy Owens wed Bennett Abell in New Salem, Illinois. Fourteen years later, about the same time Lincoln, who was living in New Salem with the Abells, was admitted to the bar, Betsy determined to make a match between her sister Mary and the newly admitted lawyer. Lincoln had met Mary three years before, and now she was coming to New Salem to stay with her sister.

Lincoln described what happened next in a letter to his friend, Mrs. Browning.

> It was, then, in the autumn of 1836 that a married lady of my acquaintance and who was a great friend of mine, being about to pay a visit to her father and other relatives in Kentucky, proposed to me that on her return she would bring a sister of hers with her on the condition that I would engage to become her brother-in-law with all convenient dispatch. I, of course, accepted the proposal, for you know I could not have done otherwise, had I really been averse to it; but privately, between you and me I was most confoundedly well pleased with the project. (Carl Sandburg, *Abraham Lincoln: The Prairie Years and the War Years*, 59)

For an ambitious lawyer, Mary Owens would have been a good catch. She was educated and came from a higher social station than Lincoln (so would the next Mary). Marrying her would have been good for his career as both an attorney and a politician. As an added bonus, if true, some accounts said Mary Owens had beauty, intelligence, and vivacity, which attracted many admirers. One would suspect, given her sister's enthusiasm about making a match between the two, that Mary was interested in Lincoln too.

So what happened?

Regarding Mary's attractiveness, though some describe her as pretty, others—well, let's just say that their views were less kind. There are claims Lincoln was disappointed in her looks. He hadn't seen her for three years, after all, which was a long time in frontier life, and during that time she had supposedly grown heavy and may have lost some teeth. Losing teeth wasn't uncommon back then since dentistry as we know it didn't become a licensed profession until the end of the nineteenth century. And it wasn't until 1885 that toothbrushes—made of boar bristles with bone, wood, or ivory handles—were mass produced in the United States, though they'd been available earlier than that in England. Whatever the case, Lincoln did propose, either because he was taken with Mary or because he felt obligated to do so.

Mary would later claim that she rejected Lincoln's proposal. Here we must remind readers that no one has ever described Lincoln as handsome, although also no one ever said he was too heavy. For his part, Lincoln claimed he only reluctantly offered to marry her. He must have been ambivalent because he wrote in one of the letters he sent her that "I should be much happier with you than the way I am, provided I saw no signs of discontent in you." In another he wrote, "What I do wish is that our further acquaintance shall depend on yourself."

Whatever happened, after the two became engaged, Lincoln moved to Springfield, where he established an office. After the move, he wrote Mary Owens again.

> I am often thinking of what we said of your coming to live in Springfield. I am afraid you would not be satisfied. There is a great deal of flourishing about in carriages here, which it would be your doom to see without shareing it. You would have to be

poor without the means of hiding your poverty. Do you believe that you could bear that patiently? Whatever woman may cast her lot with mine, should any ever do so, it is my intention to do all in my power to make her happy and contented; and there is nothing I can imagine that could make me more unhappy than to fail in that effort. I know I should be much happier with you than the way I am, provided I saw no signs of discontent in you. What you have said to me may have been in jest, or I may have misunderstood it. If so, then let it be forgotten; if otherwise, I much wish you would think seriously before you decide. For my part I have already decided. What I have said, I will most positively abide by, provided you wish it. My opinion is that you had better not do it. You have not been accustomed to hardship, and it may be more severe than you now imagine. I know you are capable of thinking correctly on any subject, and if you deliberate maturely upon this before you decide, then I am willing to abide by your decision.

Yours, &c, Lincoln.
(Reproduced in Sandburg, *Abraham Lincoln*, 57)

Reading this letter almost two hundred years later, it appears that either Lincoln was experiencing second or third thoughts about marrying Mary or he was extremely insecure and wanted reassurance that she loved him and would stand by him no matter what. We're not sure what he was trying to accomplish, but we're certain it wasn't a declaration of love designed to thrill a woman's heart.

Poverty didn't seem to be what Mary had in mind, or maybe she wanted more romance. She kindly wrote back and ended the engagement. She later told a friend that "Mr. Lincoln was deficient in those little links which make up the chain of a woman's happiness" (Wilson and Davis, *Herndon's Informants*, 256). In 1841, she would marry Jessie Vineyard. A year after that, Lincoln would marry Mary Todd, another Kentucky girl.

PLACES TO VISIT

Buffalo Trace Distillery
113 Great Buffalo Trace
Frankfort, KY
(502) 696-5926; buffalotracedistillery.com

Heaven Hill
311 Gilkey Run Road
Bardstown, KY
(502) 337-1000; www.heaven-hill.com

Jim Beam American Stillhouse
526 Happy Hollow Road
Clermont, KY
(502) 215-2295; jimbeam.com

Kentucky Lincoln Trail
kentuckylincolntrail.org

Maker's Mark Distillery
3350 Burks Spring Road
Loretto, KY
(270) 865-2881; makersmark.com

My Old Kentucky Home
501 East Stephen Foster Avenue
Bardstown, KY
(502) 348-3502; louisvillewaterfront.com

Nelson County Courthouse
Bardstown, KY
aogk.org

Old Talbott Tavern
101 West Stephen Foster Avenue
Bardstown, KY
(502) 348-3494; talbotts.com

Oscar Getz Museum of Whiskey History
Spalding Hall
114 North Fifth Street
Bardstown, KY
(502) 348-2999; whiskeymuseum.com

Sisters of Charity of Nazareth
Visitor Center
O'Connell Hall on the Nazareth
134 Main Avenue
Nazareth, KY
(502) 348-1500; scnfamily.org

Woodford Reserve Distillery
7855 McCracken Pike
Versailles, KY
(859) 879-1812; woodfordreserve.com

3

LEXINGTON, KENTUCKY

Athens of the West

LEXINGTON BELLE

When I look at photos of Mary Todd taken after Lincoln became president, I see a dour and unhappy woman, weighed down by age and care. The loveliness, animation, and happiness contemporaries ascribed to her in her youth would be drained away by tragedy—the loss of three children, her husband's assassination, and a trial and hospitalization after an emotional breakdown.

But at one time she was a beguiling belle—charming, coquettish, educated beyond most women of her day, and known for her wit, humor, and conversation. She took an avid interest in politics and came from a well-connected and well-to-do family. Her paternal grandfather was one of the founders of Lexington, Kentucky, and two men who would later run for president would vie for her hand in marriage—Abraham Lincoln and his political rival, Stephen Douglas.

The exterior of the Mary Todd Lincoln House. *Photo courtesy of Lexington Convention & Visitors Bureau*

The two-story home at 578 West Main Street where Mary lived starting at age thirteen, with its shades of red brick and black shutters, seems to foretell a bright future for a pretty, fascinating woman from an established and wealthy Lexington family—marrying well and securing a fulfilling life. As you walk through the sumptuously decorated home there are no signs of the darkness that lay ahead for Mary Todd.

THE MARY TODD LINCOLN HOUSE

The historic Mary Todd Lincoln House was built in 1806 and first operated as an inn and tavern called the Sign of the Green Tree;

The Mary Todd Lincoln House in Lexington shows how the well-to-do Todd family lived. The parlor, shown here, is where the family and guests would gather. *Photo courtesy of Lexington Convention & Visitors Bureau*

Mary's father, Robert Todd, bought the building in 1832. Mary would live there for seven years until she moved to Springfield, Illinois, but the home remained in the family until 1849 when her father died of cholera during an epidemic. Knowing he was going to die, Todd made and signed a will but didn't have it properly witnessed, and his two families fought over it—the children by his first wife, Eliza Ann Parker, which included Mary, squaring off against his second wife and her children. The property was sold at public auction.

As an aside, the Lexington home where Mary was born and lived when she was younger is now gone, but the Mary Todd Lincoln Marker at 511 West Short Street reads, "On this site

Mary Todd, wife of Abraham Lincoln, was born Dec. 13, 1818, and here spent her childhood."

I arrived in Lexington from Bardstown after a trip that took a little over an hour, admiring the scenery on the Bluegrass Parkway along the way. The Mary Todd Lincoln House juxtaposed sharply with its mixed surroundings of storefronts and offices. Stepping through the white front door into the darkened foyer of the home, I left the hot, humid August day behind. Despite the heavy velvets and rich damasks, the air seemed cooler, more bearable.

But in many ways, it's all about the contrasts. Lincoln's boyhood homes had been a series of roughly hewn one-room log cabins, sparsely furnished and with seemingly no thought given to decor. Pure function. Here was grandeur that left no surface unembellished. Ornately framed family portraits and landscapes hung on elegant patterned wallpaper; bold and richly colored carpets covered the Kentucky ash wood floors; and a pianoforte original to the family stood in a parlor where the Todds would have entertained guests. (Much of the Todd house underwent extensive renovations after falling into near ruin, and though the furniture is appropriate to the time, it's not all the Todds'.) They weren't minimalists in Mary's day, and the home has the overcrowded look that was the preferred style of the well-to-do back then. What must Lincoln have thought when he entered his wife's house for the first time and saw all the many wonderful pieces of furniture, pottery, and glassware and the fireplaces with their elaborate mantels?

Surprisingly, when it opened to the public in 1977, the Mary Todd Lincoln House was the first house museum in the country to honor a first lady. Go figure. The touches of time are always interesting for those like me who love house museums, but there are some telling features that highlight Mary's life in particular. In the tense atmosphere leading up to the Civil War, Mary's father, Robert Todd, said he was against slavery, but he owned slaves who lived in the house and waited on the family. As the Todd family ate their meals, a slave would have stood nearby

A large feather fan, seen here leaning against the fireplace, was kept in the dining room table at the Mary Todd Lincoln House in Lexington, Kentucky. Slaves used the fan to cool the family while they ate their dinner.
Photo courtesy of Lexington Convention & Visitors Bureau

fanning them. The long-handled fan they would have used now stands near the table laid with fine porcelain and silver, as if the Todds might show up at any time for dinner, which would also have been cooked by slaves. To be sure, not one of the Todds went into the kitchen to help with the cleanup.

The home, now on a busy thoroughfare, was once surrounded by thirty-two acres of land, but there's no longer a languid sylvan charm as there is, say, at Ashland, the home of Henry and Lucretia Clay, who were friends with the Todds and who often sat in their parlor being served iced mint juleps by Nelson, the Todd family's butler. There's a pretty, well-tended garden out back filled with blooming flowers. Maybe what's most telling are the portraits of Mary's siblings, several of whom died fighting for the Confederacy. That would have made for some heated dinner conversations.

Stepmom from Hell

As ideal as the fourteen-room home might look, it wasn't a happy place for Mary even before the war. She was the fourth of seven children, and before she turned seven, her mother, the former Elizabeth "Eliza" Parker, died shortly after childbirth at the age of thirty-one. Mary's father, an attorney by training, was a successful businessman and state legislator who was frequently away from home. He needed help with the children, and, within six months of his wife's death, such a short time that Lexington society was said to be shocked, he became engaged to Elizabeth "Betsey" Humphreys.

Betsey, at twenty-six, was nine years younger than Todd and was already considered a spinster. Highly educated, she was from an affluent family that was both politically and socially connected. Betsey's father had been a surgeon during the Revolutionary War and was chairman of the board of Staunton Academy. After Dr. Humphreys's death, his widow moved her family to Frankfort, Kentucky.

Mary's mother's Parker relatives especially disapproved of the widower Todd becoming engaged so quickly, which didn't help in fostering a good relationship between the Todd children and their new stepmother, who history recalls as the stepmom from hell. Betsey Humphreys's character didn't help matters. She was no Sarah Lincoln, who is credited with turning Abe and his sister from half-wild, ill-fed, and poorly clothed children living in a dirty hovel to well-scrubbed, somewhat educated (not many people in Pigeon Creek were spending a ton of time in school back then), and well-behaved children, giving them not only love but lots of guidance and structure. Betsey was imperious and condescending. No one described her as warm or comforting. Taught by her own mother to rule a household with an iron hand, she didn't understand that grieving children might need more than strict rules. She also had a somewhat antiquated belief (at least it seems so in this day and age) that it took seven generations to produce a "lady." Observing the Todd girls, she must have thought a few more generations were needed.

To give her full due, Betsey Humphreys Todd may have been a little tired as well. Not only did she have a pack of stepchildren to care for, including a baby, she and Robert Todd would have nine children of their own between 1827 and 1841. Even with my poor math skills, that adds up to at least nine births (we don't know if there were miscarriages in between or after the youngest was born) in fourteen years. That poor woman was pretty much pregnant for a decade and a half. Sadly, each set of Todd children, by wives one and two, had a Robert who died shortly after birth.

Betsey preferred her own brood to those from her husband's first marriage, but we'll cut her some slack. Going from spinster to mother and stepmother in charge of enough children to field a baseball team, even living in a large, elegant home with slaves to take care of all the chores, must have been overwhelming. Children would have been everywhere.

GRATZ PARK

Mary seems to have tried to escape the pandemonium, as well as her stepmother's dislike, through education. She first attended the institution known as Dr. Ward's Academy, founded in 1827 by Reverend John Ward, an Episcopalian minister. Mary graduated in 1831. Tuition at Ward's was forty-four dollars per year, with French lessons extra. Mary, by the way, spoke excellent French. Located at 190 Market Street and built around 1794, the academy building is now known as the Ridgley House and is the oldest home still standing in historic Gratz Park, about a six-minute car ride from Mary's house via West Vine and South Limestone Streets.

Surrounded by historic homes, including those of Confederate general John Hunt Morgan and Union loyalist Thomas Bodley, Gratz Park, which opens onto the campus of Transylvania University, is a lovely introduction to Lexington history. As an example of Kentucky courtliness, it's said that when Mrs. Hunt was surrounded by an angry mob at the farmers' market during the war, Mr. Bullock kindly escorted her to safety. Nearby, in the historic Gratz Park Inn, the restaurant Distilled at Gratz Park celebrates Lexington's culinary heritage.

John Hunt Morgan, dashing, daring, and impulsive, invaded Indiana (against his superior's orders, of course) and fought the only Civil War battle in that state. Morgan attended Transylvania University, just a couple blocks from his home on West Third Street and North Upper Street. As a student, being Morgan, he was reprimanded for dueling. He was always a rule breaker, which ultimately led to his demise but also made him very attractive to the ladies. Other Transylvania alums include a roster of who was who in the eighteenth and nineteenth centuries, such as General George Rogers Clark, Governor Isaac Shelby, Henry Clay, Cassius M. Clay, and James Lane Allen. Mary's father, Robert S. Todd, was also a Transylvania alum.

Founded in 1780, Transylvania is Kentucky's oldest university. The Greek Revival–style Old Morrison, Transylvania's second administration building, features large steps leading up to a raised main floor and massive Doric columns. Built circa 1833, it was seized by the Union Army and used as a hospital during the Civil War; as the fortunes of war shifted, it served as a place for both the Union and Confederate armies to bivouac. But not, you know, at the same time.

Also part of the beautiful Gratz Park neighborhood is the Bodley-Bullock Home at 200 Market Street—just across the park green from the Hunt-Morgan House. General Thomas Bodley, a hero of the War of 1812 and an attorney, paid $10,000 for the house around 1814. A grand house with gorgeous restored gardens and the finest example of a cantilevered elliptical staircase in any Kentucky Federal-style house, it served as the headquarters for Union troops during the Civil War and was also where the pro-Union newspaper the *Mail Bag* was published.

One of the few early professional buildings still in existence, Henry Clay's Law Office (circa 1803) can be seen from the upstairs windows of the Hunt-Morgan House. Clay practiced law

The lovely gardens of the
Hunt-Morgan House in
Gratz Park in Lexington.
*Photo courtesy of
Jane Simon Ammeson*

Union troops used the Federal-style Bodley-Bullock House in historic Gratz Park as headquarters during the Civil War, and Confederate troops did for a brief time as well.

here until 1910 when he embarked upon a very successful political career and just barely lost the presidency in 1844 (Lincoln campaigned for him). It was most likely here that Clay met with his client Aaron Burr, who in 1806 was accused of hatching an extraordinary plot.

Of Colonel Burr

Important Communications—By a Gentleman of the highest respectability from Kentucky we are furnished with the following intelligence.

Poughkeepsie Journal (Poughkeepsie, NY), Tuesday, December 2, 1806

The United States District Court of Kentucky district having commenced their November session following the substance of an affidavit of Joseph Hamilton Davies, Esq. attorney general for the United States which was made before the judge of the court, to wit:

That Aaron Burr, Esq., late vice-president of the United States, had formed an Association for making war against Spain, invading Mexico and forming a Distinct Empire in the western country that he was raising forces and purchasing up the necessary provisions and stores for the purpose.

It was reported that Col. Burr was in Lexington at the time the motion was made and that he had notice of the transaction three hours after it was made.

Clay believed Burr was innocent when he took on his case but shunned him later when he discovered the truth. As for Burr, well, knowing his history, what else could one expect? The guy was certainly a rogue . . . and gone rogue as well.

LEXINGTON CEMETERY

After graduating from Dr. Ward's Academy, and being unhappy at home, Mary Todd decided to board at Madame Mentelle's School for Young Ladies. Although Madame Mentelle's was very close to her family's elegant home, Mary spent the week at school, going home only on the weekends. Charlotte Victoire LeClere Mentelle was Paris born, and her school, where tuition ran $120 a month ($2345.63 today), taught French, poetry, comportment, conversation, and dancing—a necessity for young women of Mary's status. Quite the woman, Madame Mentelle was the daughter of a French physician who, upon his wife's death, raised his only child in a very strict, almost abusive fashion. To cure her of a fear of death, he locked her in a room overnight with the dead body of a family acquaintance. She and her husband escaped France during the bloody French Revolution and had eight children, seven of whom died before Madame. She and her husband ran their very popular school together and lived to be almost ninety. Madame Mentelle also provided more of a home life for Mary Todd than her father and stepmother. In another interesting connection to the Lincoln family, Madame Mentelle's daughter Mary married Thomas Hart Clay, the son of Henry Clay, who would become Abe's good friend.

Madame Mentelle is buried at the 170-acre Lexington Cemetery, as are many other residents of Gratz Park, such as John Hunt Morgan and his father, John Wesley Hunt; Henry and Lucretia Clay; and many members of Mary's family, including her paternal grandparents, her father, her mother, four of her siblings, and her three children. Standing in the center of the cemetery is a monument to Henry Clay. Other monuments include the Confederate Soldier Monument and the Ladies' Confederate Memorial.

The cemetery was founded in 1849, partly as a place to bury the victims of the cholera epidemic of that year (some eight hundred would be buried there before the year was out, including Mary's father, who fell victim to the disease). Also buried there is the unlikely hero of the 1833 cholera epidemic, William "King" Solomon, who, according to the Lexington History Museum in a scandalous story that I love, claimed to be the son of a rich Virginian planter who had been friends with Henry Clay when young. Migrating to Lexington, he took up drinking big time and was in and out of jail so many times after being found passed out in the streets that a judge decided to sell him as a servant for a term of nine months. A free black woman known as Aunt Charlotte, vendor of homemade cakes and pies, purchased him for fifty cents (the Lexington Cemetery website reports it was eighteen cents). He essentially became a white man enslaved to a black woman—don't you love it? History is full of quirks like that and interesting asides, which again gives us a window into the world as it was back then.

Solomon seems to have had a good heart and a sense of humor. When an opponent of Clay's offered a free drink in return for a vote, Solomon agreed and downed the drink. When the man saw Solomon later that day and asked if he'd kept his part of the deal, Solomon said no, adding, "You may have been foolish enough to try to bribe me, but I'm not foolish enough to vote for you."

When the 1833 cholera epidemic ravaged Lexington, Solomon said he was immune because he drank whiskey, not the water from the infected wells. Aunt Charlotte died of the illness, as did three of the city's doctors. Those who could leave did, and even gravediggers decided not to work.

Not Solomon, who for two months worked day and night burying corpses at the Old Episcopal Burying Ground on Third Street, which helped keep the disease from spreading. That same year, when the fall court session began, the judge (we don't know if it was the same judge who indentured him to Aunt Charlotte) noticed Solomon in the back of the room. Stepping down from the bench, the judge walked to where Solomon sat and held out his hand in honor of what Solomon had done for the community. Everyone else in the courtroom then stood as well, shaking hands with the hard-drinking gravedigger. Upon his death in 1854, Solomon was buried in the then new Lexington Cemetery, and a statue declaring him a hero was erected at the gravesite. Solomon lived to be seventy-nine years old despite his drinking and burying of infected corpses.

Sadly, on September 11, 1861, Benjamin Gratz, one of the cemetery's founders, for whom Gratz Park was named, had the overwhelmingly heart-wrenching job of burying his son there—Union Army captain Cary Gist Gratz, who had died a month earlier from the wounds suffered during the Battle of Wilson's Creek near Springfield, Missouri. Before the war was over, the cemetery would become the resting place for 964 more Union soldiers, both white and black, and over 102 Confederates.

Like many families during the Civil War, the Todd household was indeed a family divided. Mary would go on to marry the Great Emancipator. The husband of Emile Todd Helm (Mary's youngest half-sister), General Benjamin Hardin Helm, was killed fighting for the Confederates at Chickamauga. Sam Todd,

Mary's half-brother, was killed fighting for the Confederates at Shiloh. David Todd, another Confederate half-brother, was wounded at Vicksburg and died after the war in 1867. Aleck Todd, yet another Confederate half-brother, died in a skirmish near Baton Rouge. Mary's full brother George Rogers Clark Todd was a surgeon at a Confederate hospital in Camden, South Carolina. Levi Todd, a full brother to Mary, was a Unionist but was too old and unfit for military duty during the Civil War. He died in 1864. Mary's only other full brother, Robert Parker Todd, was long since dead.

Of the fourteen living Todd children at the time of the Civil War, eight supported the Confederacy, and six supported the Union. Supposedly when Mary was asked about the death of her half-brothers while fighting against Union soldiers, she replied that it was hard for her to feel sorrow because if they had been successful they would have been part of a mob that would have pulled her husband from the White House and murdered him.

ASHLAND

When Mary Todd was young, it's said she rode her pony to Ashland, the home of Henry Clay, and told the guests at his dinner party she would enjoy living in the White House some-day. We don't know if she rode cross-country, but today you can get from the Mary Todd Lincoln House to Ashland, located in Lexington's historic Ashland Park, in seven minutes, taking West Main southeast where it curves and turns into West Vine Street.

Though it's likely given the friendship between the two families that Mary visited Ashland, there's an ongoing, two-century-long debate among historians about whether Lincoln ever did. Lincoln, a great admirer of Clay, campaigned for him in southwestern Indiana in 1844 when he was running for the presidency, but his support of Clay is said to have waned after he met the great statesman following a speech he gave in

Once a large estate and working farm, Ashland, the home of
Henry Clay, is now surrounded by the city of Lexington.
Photo courtesy of Lexington Convention & Visitors Bureau

Lexington in 1847. Lincoln was visiting Mary's family at the
time. I wasn't there, but I'm going with the researchers who believe Lincoln was invited to dine with the Clays during the visit.

Designated a national historic landmark, the eighteen-room
Clay mansion was built in 1812. Part of the house was designed
by architect Benjamin Henry Latrobe, who also designed the
United States Capitol. Originally an estate of six hundred acres,
the property is now down to twenty acres, still a large chunk
of land in what is now the city and just a few miles from downtown. The home, which is open for tours, displays Clay family
belongings and memorabilia. There's a gated English parterre
garden and several outbuildings, including the Keeper's Cottage
and the ice-house and dairy-cellar system, that dot the prettily

landscaped grounds. The remains of the slave quarters (yes, Clay owned slaves) have been discovered and are being restored.

Ashland was gracious home but the *New-England Farmer and Horticultural Register* describe Clay's estate as a working farm.

> There is a stone cheese-house and a stone butter house, Ashland being celebrated for the quantity and quality of butter made thereat. His chicken-house, dove-house, stables, barns and sheds, are all in perfect repair, spacious, neat, and in order. There is also a large green house filled with choice plants and beautiful flowers. His fruit and vegetable garden contains about four acres, and in its arrangement and cultivation, I saw Mrs. Clay giving personal directions.
>
> His Negro cottages are exceedingly comfortable, all white washed, clean and well furnished, and plenty of flowers in the windows about the dwellings. (vol. 24, "Henry Clay's Farm," 89)

According to Ashland curator Eric Brooks, the Clays raised pigs, and Henry's wife, Lucretia, was known for her hams that sold at Lexington's downtown market, which still exists. Though you can no longer taste her hams, Ashland's brick smokehouse has been converted into the charming Ginkgo Tree Café, offering a way to dine on the estate.

OTHER TRACES FROM MARY'S TIME

Lexington was known as the "Athens of the West," but even with its beauty, refinement, and proximity to free states, slavery was still legal. In 1833, Kentucky legislators passed a nonimportation act, prohibiting slaves from being brought into the state. A good step, I guess. But it didn't stop them from being bought or sold in Kentucky, and by the 1840s, the city was considered the center of the state's slave trade. At what's now the northwest corner of Courthouse Square, African Americans were sold at the market's Slave Auction Block, including those "belonging" to the Robert Todd estate after his death. A whipping post was also located there to use on those who violated the city's regulations and rules. Fun times back then. Now the site of a busy farmer's market, the square is a seven-minute drive from Ashland heading northwest on East High Street.

There are other reminders of Mary's time in Lexington. These sites can be found on the Lincoln's Lexington Walking Tour and include Giron's Confectionery, located at 125 North Mill Street. Don't bother to stop as it's not a candy store anymore, although the building is still there. Swiss immigrant Mathurin Giron opened his store here sometime after 1810 and built the edifice now standing in 1837. One of Mary's relatives recalled her purchasing confections there, and the recipe for the white almond cake she was famous for making (it was said to be her husband's favorite) is attributed to Giron.

Nearby is the building that housed Cassius Clay's printing office at North Mill Street between Main Street and Short Street. Clay, a friend of the Todd family, opened the shop in 1845 and printed an emancipationist newspaper there, but when Clay left the office empty during an illness, proslavery forces took apart his equipment. Clay was considered as a running mate for Lincoln in 1860, and when Abe was elected president, he appointed Clay ambassador to Russia.

Lexington's oldest surviving post office was built in 1836. Located at 307 West Short Street, it's easy to suppose that Mary Todd and Abraham Lincoln might have mailed their letters here. In an interesting twist of history, Joseph Ficklin, who was Lexington's postmaster in 1836, lived not too far away on High Street, where he had a young boarder named Jefferson Davis.

Known as Robards' Headquarters, the series of buildings located at 514–522 West Short Street were occupied by slave trader Lewis Robards, who held slave sales in one building and showed female slaves in another. Mary's brother Levi lived across the street in the old Todd home during this period. On the same block, at 511 Short Street, was the home of Mary's maternal grandmother, Elizabeth Parker. Mary was close to her grandmother, who tried to help her grandchildren deal with their stepmother. Known as Parker Place, the facade of the home here dates back to 1871. Parker died in 1850 (her husband had died half a century earlier), and Lincoln came to Lexington that spring to help settle her estate. His duties included freeing three of her slaves.

PLACES TO VISIT

Ashland
120 Sycamore Road
Lexington, KY 40502
(859) 266-8581

Bodley-Bullock House
200 Market Street
Lexington, KY
(859) 252-8014
https://www.lexjrleague.com/?nd=bodley_bullock_house

Ginkgo Tree Café
1305 Fincastle Road
Lexington, KY
(859) 230-1953
https://www.facebook.com/ginkgotreecafe/

Henry Clay's Law Office
176 North Mill Street
Lexington, KY

Hunt-Morgan House
201 North Mill Street
Lexington, KY
https://www.bluegrasstrust.org/history/

John Hunt Morgan Trail
https://www.hhhills.org/John-Hunt-Morgan.html
trailsrus.com/morgan

Lexington Cemetery
833 West Main Street
Lexington, KY
(859) 255-5522

Lexington Farmers' Market
199 South Broadway
Lexington, KY
(859) 608-2655
https://www.lexingtonfarmersmarket.com

"Lincolns' Lexington" Walking Tour
https://www.mtlhouse.org/related-links/

Mary Todd Lincoln House
578 West Main Street
Lexington, KY 40507
(859) 233-9999
https://www.mtlhouse.org

Mary Todd Lincoln Marker
511 West Short Street
Lexington, KY

Transylvania University
300 North Broadway
Lexington, KY
(859) 233-8300
www.transy.edu

Ward's Academy
190 Market Street
Lexington, KY

4

SOUTHEASTERN INDIANA TRAILS

HARRISON COUNTY, INDIANA: CORYDON, A LINCOLN HOME, AND SQUIRE BOONE'S CAVERNS

The Lincoln exodus from Kentucky began when Josiah Lincoln and his family crossed the Ohio River into Harrison County, Indiana. Their path most likely would have led them through Mauckport, past where Squire and Jane Boone and four of their grown children had settled on Buck Creek in 1804, establishing the first grain mill in the county. The Lincolns (and earlier the Boones) would have made the river passage by flatboat or as passengers on the state's first ferry, operated by John Peter Mauck. Mauck's ferry, at first just a raft and towline from Brandenburg, Kentucky, to Mauckport, Indiana, started operating as early as 1808 and maybe before.

For a brief period Mauckport prospered because of its proximity to the capital in Corydon farther north. Time hasn't been kind to Mauckport, though, and according to the 2010 census

Corydon was the capital of the Northwest Territory and served as the capital of Indiana until 1825. Now open to the public, the former capitol building sits on the historic courthouse square in downtown Corydon. *Photo courtesy of Jane Simon Ammeson*

the town had only fifty inhabitants. But time has made it easier for me to follow Josiah's footsteps: instead of using a raft and towline or a flatboat, I drive along Kentucky Route 79 through Brandenburg, Kentucky, and cross the Matthew E. Welsh Bridge into Mauckport. There the road becomes Indiana State Road 135, which leads north into the town of Corydon, fifteen miles away.

Abraham Lincoln's uncle Josiah was the middle child—the one who ran to get help after his father was shot on the family farm and who ended up penniless when Mordecai inherited their father's estate. Shortly after the War of 1812 a large part of Indiana territory became available for settlement, and

Josiah left Kentucky to established a farm on 160 acres in Blue River Township, near Depauw and Corydon, in what would become Harrison County when Indiana became a state in 1816. Founded in 1808 and now the Harrison County seat, Corydon was first the capital of the Northwest Territories from 1813 to 1816, and then Indiana's state capital from 1816 until 1825. In 1825 Indiana's capital was moved to the more centrally located Indianapolis.

The Kintner House Inn

Parking off Corydon's charming town square, where the original state capitol building still stands, I climb the steps leading to the porch of the Kintner House Inn, a place where Josiah hung out back in the early 1800s. "People can walk in here and feel like guests must have felt over a hundred years ago," Dee Windell, the Kintner House's innkeeper, tells me.

Indeed, sitting in the elaborately decorated Victorian-style parlor and looking through lace curtains out onto the front lawn, one can almost hear the horse hooves pounding the road outside, the rustle of crinoline as women walk up the stairs, and the banter of men as they drink in what was at first called the Kintner Tavern. Built by Jacob Kintner, a harness and saddle maker (a big business back then), it was the perfect place to stop for travelers visiting the seat of power. One such guest was Josiah Lincoln, says Allison Carney, who also works at the Kintner House Inn. And it wasn't just Uncle Josiah who passed through the area: Thomas, Nancy, Sarah, and Abe followed Josiah across the river four years later. Squire and Jane Boone and their family—and even John Hunt Morgan and his Raiders—would all cross the Ohio River into Indiana and end up in Corydon or Harrison County at various times.

Around 1819, Kintner opened his two-story limestone home to travelers, and as business boomed, he decided to go ritzy and built an elegant new hotel. Fire destroyed that one, and in 1873 he tried again with the Kintner House Inn, which still stands today. The exterior is so pretty that it was featured on

The historic Kintner House Inn, Corydon, Indiana. When Morgan took the town of Corydon during his Civil War raid into Indiana, he stayed at the Kintner House to celebrate his victory. Tom Lincoln's brother Josiah also visited after he moved to Harrison County, Indiana.
Photo courtesy of Jane Simon Ammeson

two Hallmark Christmas cards, and the inside is suffused with Victorian-era charm, including both an organ and a piano in the parlor and bedrooms with fringed lampshades, tasseled curtains, and antiques such as an eight-foot-tall flame mahogany armoire, a walnut dresser with a pink marble top, an inlaid star-patterned game table, and an eight-foot-tall walnut bed hand carved in the 1850s.

The Lincolns of Harrison County

The direct descendants of Abraham Lincoln died out with the death of his great-grandson, Robert Todd Lincoln Beckwith, on December 24, 1985. But Josiah did much better in the genetic lottery, and many of his relatives, some with the last name of Lincoln, still populate Indiana. In an October 2012 article titled "Lincoln Like Me," Lincoln descendant Megan Fernandez, an editor at *Indianapolis Monthly*, points out that the Lincolns of Harrison County are now among the closest living kin of the greatest American president. She also shares family lore that Thomas Lincoln and his family visited his older brother's home on their way further west to Perry (now Spencer) County.

"In the 1930s, officials in Corydon, the Harrison County seat, campaigned for the construction of a Lincoln Highway to connect the president's heritage sites in Kentucky, Indiana, and Illinois, and it would have passed through Mom's tiny hometown, Milltown, and Dad's tinier one, Depauw, to demark what is believed to be a path Abraham once traveled with his family as a boy," writes Fernandez. "The exact route was just hearsay, but several locals, including Dad's grandfather, gave certified testimony to prove it, based on an oral history otherwise lost to time."

In a letter published in the *Indianapolis Star* on August 13, 1931, J. L. Summers of Milltown, Indiana, writes that documents point "to the fact that Thomas Lincoln crossed the Ohio River at Boones Ford, south of Corydon, and landed in the Boone Settlement, he being acquainted with and related to the

Boones in Harrison County, who had come before and settled there." Summers goes on to say there are affidavits showing that Thomas traveled to where Josiah lived and spent a few days there before moving on to Jasper, Indiana (the Enlows, who owned a mill there, were said to have been neighbors of the Lincolns in Kentucky), and then to Little Pigeon Creek.

Summers recalled a long-told family story that when Thomas Lincoln and his family were staying at Josiah's home, they swapped horses. True to Thomas's luck, the horse he left at his brother's home turned out to be one of the best in Josiah's stable.

Fernandez is what I call a double Lincoln. She and Abe are first cousins five times removed—and doubly so. That's because her mother, Darlene Lincoln Briscoe, the daughter of Jesse Lincoln, is a descendant of Josiah and Catherine Barlow Lincoln. Their daughter, Nancy, who was born in Blue River Township, Harrison County, in 1810, married John Briscoe in 1827. Before her death in 1843, Nancy and John had six children. Three died in childhood; a surviving son, Anthony Wayne, married Margaret Jane Soppenfield. More than a century later, one of their descendants, Anthony Ware Briscoe, married Darlene Lincoln, now Darlene Brisco, and the couple had seven children—Fernandez being their youngest.

"We never really talked about Lincoln," says Fernandez. "My father didn't even know he was a Lincoln. My great-great grandfather on Dad's side, who fought in the Civil War with General Sherman, mentions President Lincoln in his diary, but never their kinship." This branch of the Lincoln family is overlooked not only by their own family members but also other's interested in Lincoln history. When Fernandez visited the Lincoln home in Springfield, Illinois, she was told to stand in line with the rest of the visitors when she tried to share her family heritage.

Josiah's Blue River Township farm, long since sold, is once again owned by a family member, and an old barn dating back to his time still stands. Josiah is buried in the Blue River Church

Cemetery in Depauw along with other members of the Lincoln family. The Blue River Church that still stands near the cemetery may date back to that time. "It's a little hard to find," says Briscoe, who offers to show me the way to Josiah's gravesite and to the old—and now new—family farm. "I think people interested in Lincoln would want to know more about Josiah's family." There are so many relatives on this family tree that Briscoe says you can't throw a walnut in Harrison County without hitting a Lincoln descendant.

Morgan's Raiders Raid Corydon

Josiah wasn't the only visitor to the Kintner Inn connected to Abe Lincoln. During the Civil War, Confederate general John Hunt Morgan and some 2,400 of his troops defied his commanding officer's orders and crossed the Ohio River from Kentucky into southeastern Indiana. Morgan and his men thundered past the settlement founded by Squire Boone—brother of Daniel and interconnected to the Lincolns by marriage and generations of friendships—to fight the only Civil War battle in Indiana. Morgan's Raiders defeated 450 badly outnumbered members of the Indiana Home Guard at the Battle of Corydon, which is listed, along with Gettysburg, as one of only two Civil War battle sites on Northern soil. During the hour-long battle, four of the home guard were killed, several were wounded, and three hundred and thirty-five were captured; the remaining men escaped. Of the Confederate soldiers, eight were killed and thirty-three wounded. Morgan released his captives upon entering the town of Corydon, but he and his men plundered homes and stores and collected ransoms, including $690 from the county treasurer, $600 each from the city's two best stores, and $700 to $1000 from three mills on the promise not to burn them to the ground.

Morgan and his officers also took the time to raise the Confederate flag (it was taken down as soon as he left town) and turned the Kintner House Inn into his temporary headquarters. There, his celebratory mood must have taken a hard hit when

Miss Sallie, the innkeeper's twenty-year-old daughter, showing a lot of sass, informed Morgan that the Confederates had been defeated at Gettysburg.

Done looting the city, Morgan and his men rode on, rampaging through southeast Indiana and into Ohio, where he was captured, escaped, and was finally killed by a Union soldier the night before another battle. The journey he took through Indiana and later Ohio is called the John Hunt Morgan Trail, and those who want to follow his travels can download a map to do just that. The Battle of Corydon Memorial Park is listed on the National Register of Historic Places and features a restored log cabin.

Squire Boone Caverns: Saved by a Cave

In 1790, during one of his forays into southern Indiana, Squire Boone, being chased by angry Shawnees and about to be captured, took a leap and tumbled through a waterfall into a magnificent set of caverns with underground cascades and rushing rivers just a few miles north of the Ohio River. More than one million gallons of water a day flow through what is now known as Squire Boone Caverns, creating a magical and mystical quality that you can see and feel when touring the caves. Squire credited the caverns with saving his life and thought they had spiritual qualities.

A decade or so later, when Squire lost his lands—and almost his life—in Kentucky, he and his wife, Jane, and four of their grown children crossed the Ohio and moved a few miles north to the land above the cave, establishing a village and a grain mill. Squire often spent time in his cave, reveling in the sense of awe he felt there. On the foundation stones of his mill, he carved the following inscription: "My God my life hath much befriended, I'll praise Him till my days are ended."

And well he should have given thanks. Honored by Congress for his service during the Revolutionary War, Boone often found himself in hand-to-hand combat, including during the Battle

Squire Boone's settlement, now known as Squire Boone Cavern and Zipline, includes restored historic buildings such as the old grain mill he built in 1809. *Photo courtesy of Jane Simon Ammeson*

of Fort Boonesborough. All this fighting resulted in him being wounded eleven times, and a few of these wounds were nearly fatal. Before Boone died in 1815, at age seventy-one, he asked his children to bury him in one of the passageways of the cave system under the village. And so they did.

His bones were discovered in the 1970s and a coffin was reconstructed and moved to a more protected location, but he remains where he wanted to be—in his beloved cave. Open now for visitors, Squire Boone Caverns are a popular tourist attraction. Tours pass through the series of caves with their cascading waters and include a stop in the chapel room where Squire's casket and bones rest. Above ground, the mill Squire and his family erected has been rebuilt and is grinding grain as it did two centuries ago. In the stores, costumed interpreters demonstrate skills from back in the day, such as soap and candle making, much as they would have done in Squire's time.

Besides the Kintner House Inn and the first state capitol, several other buildings in Corydon date back to the early 1800s and the times of Boone, Lincoln, and Morgan, including the Governor's Mansion and the Old Treasury Building (Indiana's first state office building), which were built in 1817, and the Colonel Thomas Lloyd Posey home, among others. Corydon's Grand Masonic Lodge, the first in the state, was built in 1819.

MADISON, INDIANA: HISTORIC HOMES AND CIVIL WAR CONNECTIONS

Emilie Todd Travels North

From Corydon, if that's the way he came, Thomas Lincoln would travel west to arrive at his new homestead in Little Pigeon Creek, but another Lincoln family connection can be discovered by following State Road 135 north to State Road 56 east on the seventy-two-mile trip to Madison, which may be the prettiest of the Indiana port cities on the Ohio. Founded in 1809, Madison was a nexus for the busy steamboat traffic that once plied the river and was later connected to the Midwest via trains. The city's glorious past remains spectacularly on display—it possesses the largest historic district in Indiana, with over 1,500 nineteenth-century structures. The architectural styles include Second Empire, Victorian, Georgian, and Federal, and 133 blocks of the city are listed on the National Register of Historic Places.

A beautiful city, with charming southern accents such as wrought-iron gates opening onto blooming gardens and streets lined with glossy-leafed magnolia trees, Madison, in many ways, seems unchanged from when Mary Todd Lincoln's half-sister Emilie Todd Helm moved there in 1866. Crossing the Ohio River from Kentucky, the recently widowed Emilie settled into a home at 610 West Main, where she supported herself and her family by giving piano lessons.

Dorothy Darnall Jones, who penned a short biography of Helm after being a docent in her house, shares an interesting

anecdote about how the war sometimes blew things apart and put them back together in unexpected ways: "As an Episcopalian, I had always heard that Emilie Todd Helm on her first visit to Christ Episcopalian Church at Third and Mulberry had picked up her very own Book of Common Prayer in the pew rack. Union troops ransacked houses in the South and perhaps someone found her book and left it at Christ Episcopal Church." Helm was the organist at the church as well, although some weren't happy about that because of her Confederate ties and enduring Southern sympathies. The church, built in 1850, still stands and is open to the public.

According to Jones, Emilie's Greek Revival–style home, which is now privately owned, was built around 1850. Facing west, the house stood near the Union Brewery, which was destroyed by fire in 1939. The brewery was owned by the Weber family, who lived in the large brick home next-door to Helm. Both houses are still lovely and beautifully landscaped with a large magnolia tree in the front.

Emilie lived in Madison from 1866 until 1874. She first set up housekeeping at 116 Presbyterian Avenue on the north side between West and Poplar, which is now a part of King's Daughters Hospital. At both her homes in Madison Emilie lived with her mother—and Mary's hated stepmother—Elizabeth Humphreys Todd, and had three children of her own: Alexander, Elodie, and Katherine. Elizabeth died on February 14, 1874, while the family was still residing in Madison, and her funeral was held at 610 West Main, although she was buried in the Todd family lot in Lexington, Kentucky. According to Jones, Elizabeth's will, which was probated in Jefferson County, left a generous portion to Emilie, her only daughter left a widow. After her mother's death, Emilie returned to Elizabethtown, where Abraham Lincoln's only surviving child, Robert Todd Lincoln, offered her the position of postmistress.

Facing, A moss-covered angel sits pensively on a timeworn stone wall outside a home Emilie Todd Helm may well have known during her time in Madison, Indiana. *Photo courtesy of Jane Simon Ammeson*

The Greek Revival Lanier Mansion is among the most beautiful of the many historic buildings that give Madison its period feel. *Photo courtesy of Jane Simon Ammeson*

The Lanier Mansion

Madison has many other Civil War ties. Standing on the rise above the Ohio River, the apricot-colored Lanier Mansion, built in 1844, with its two-story white Corinthian columns, octagonal cupola, and unique interior features, such as curved doors that fit into rounded walls, is considered one of the best surviving examples of Greek Revival architecture in the country, according the Indiana State Museum.

James Franklin Doughty Lanier was a successful businessman responsible for the first railroad line being built in Indiana. Brave and resourceful, Lanier once packed more than one million dollars in currency and gold in his saddlebags and rode from Madison to Washington, DC, to help prevent a nationwide financial panic.

Lanier was totally Union and provided major financial contributions toward Indiana's war effort. When the Civil War broke out in 1861, the State of Indiana was facing bankruptcy.

The view from the formal gardens of the apricot-colored Lanier Mansion looking out over the Ohio River. The mansion was restored with careful attention to color and historical detail in the 1990s. *Photo courtesy of Wikimedia*

Indiana governor Oliver Morton, in answer to President Abraham Lincoln's call for troops and supplies, personally approached Lanier asking for money. Lanier's reply was to offer a $400,000 loan at 8 percent interest to help equip Indiana's volunteer troops. Later he gave a second unsecured loan of $640,000, which went toward paying interest on Indiana's debt. Besides that, in 1865 and 1868, Lanier worked abroad convincing European investors of the United States' financial stability. Though Lanier viewed the loans as his patriotic duty and eschewed any guarantees, the State of Indiana repaid his line of credit, with interest, by 1870.

Now open for tours, the Lanier home, with its handmade wallpaper, spacious rooms, high ceilings, and stunning architectural detail, is a perfect preservation of a Madison home at the time when the nation was at war and Emilie Todd Helm lived in the city.

An especially fine example of Madison's architectural legacy, the Judge Jeremiah Sullivan House dates back to the early 1800s.
Photo courtesy of Jane Simon Ammeson

The Judge Jeremiah Sullivan House

Just a few streets over and also open to the public is the Judge Jeremiah Sullivan House, now a house museum. The Virginia-born Sullivan arrived in Madison in 1816 as he was starting a family and setting up a law practice. He became involved in politics, serving in the state legislature, and sitting on the Indiana Supreme Court. Hanover College and the Indiana Historical Society count Sullivan as a founder, and he has also been credited with naming the city of Indianapolis.

Built in 1818 and located at 304 West Second Street, the Judge Jeremiah Sullivan House is considered one of the best examples of Federal-style architecture in the Old Northwest Territory. The house, where the Sullivan family lived for more than seventy years, features both a serving kitchen and a cooking kitchen in the basement with a brick floor and stone fireplace.

Madison, like many cities and towns during the Civil War, was a city divided, and the children of Charlotte and Jeremiah Sullivan were no exception. Of their seven children who survived to adulthood, two took opposing sides during the war. Algernon Sullivan became a lawyer, married a native Virginian, and established a legal practice in New York. He was sympathetic to the Confederacy.

Algernon's younger brother Jeremiah "Jerry" Sullivan Jr. graduated from the United States Naval Academy in 1848, and when President Lincoln called for volunteers, Jerry helped organize the Sixth Indiana Volunteers and led the infantry regiment as a captain. Governor Oliver Morton later appointed Sullivan as colonel of the Thirteenth Indiana, which helped defeat Stonewall Jackson at the Battle of Kernstown in March 1862. After this, Jerry Sullivan was commissioned as brigadier general, saw battle in Iuka and Corinth, Mississippi, and served as acting inspector general for Ulysses S. Grant.

HISTORIC SIDE TRIP: SPRING MILL'S PIONEER VILLAGE TAKES YOU BACK 150 YEARS

Those interested in traveling from Madison to the Lincoln Boyhood National Memorial in Lincoln City, Indiana, can stop in Lawrence County, famed for its limestone quarries, for being the home of three astronauts—Virgil "Gus" Grissom, Kenneth D. Bowersox, and Charles D. Walker—and for its Persimmon Festival, which celebrates that popular southern Indiana fruit. The absolutely delightful 1300-acre Spring Mill State Park is also along the way, with its caves, riding trails, inn, woods, and—best of all—its fascinating Pioneer Village.

Of course, all this is wonderful, but there's also a fascinating and little-known connection to Lincoln here. No, he never visited, at least as far as we know. But it so happens that Emilie Todd Helm wasn't the only half-sibling of Mary Todd to venture into Indiana. The cabin belonging to Andrew Todd, Mary's half-brother, is one of the twenty early nineteenth-century buildings preserved in Spring Mill's Pioneer Village, which also includes an apothecary, a mercantile store, a school, and other residences.

Founded in 1814, Spring Mill was once a booming place, and the centerpiece of commercial life was the three-story gristmill, built in 1817. Spring Mill's tavern and distillery were conveniently located where the stagecoach stopped on its way to Vincennes. At one time the corn, pork, and whiskey produced here was shipped downriver all the way to New Orleans, on flatboats from trees felled from the forest and cut at the village sawmill. The historic gardens have been meticulously restored, and the mill continues to grind grain; the river flowing down the millrace drives the wheel that turns the corn into meal.

One of the log cabins—a rather fancy affair with a middle area open for wagons to pull in—belonged to a true pioneer, Sally Cummins White, known in later years as Granny White. She was the type of woman who took in orphans and fed the poor. She lived to a great age even by today's standards, dying at ninety-four. And what she survived during those ninety-four years is amazing. American born, she moved to Canada and then made her way back here at age thirty-five. On the journey to Indiana, her husband died, leaving her with six small children. Granny White continued on, burying him along the way, and made her way to the middle of Indiana, where she met and married David White. According to the commemorative sign in the two-story log house that her husband built in 1824, they rode to Canada on horseback for their honeymoon. Three more children came along, and White, now the mother of nine, also tended to the destitute and ill and invited the Native Americans who made their way along the nearby Indian trail into her home. Visitors to the village can stay at the Spring Mill Inn where the desserts they serve are scrumptious, and many of them come with their own special story, including Granny White's Orchard Cake.

But what may be most curious about Pioneer Village to those interested in President Lincoln is its tie-in with our Mary. The log cabin belonging to Andrew and Mary Elizabeth Todd, built in 1830, was moved to the park one hundred years later and is known as the Munson home, named after a family that lived in the village but whose home and leather shop were too damaged to be used when the park was created.

Like the Lincolns, there are also still Todds in Indiana, including (though he's currently a partner in a Washington, DC, law firm) Charles Todd Richardson, the great-great-great-grandson of Andrew and Mary, who grew up in Bedford, a city about ten miles north of Mitchell and 15 miles from Spring Mill State Park. Richardson is related to Mary through two different descendants. His great-great-great-grandfather David Todd (1791–1852) and Mary Todd Lincoln's father, Robert Smith Todd (1791–1849), were second cousins, and his great-great-great-great-great-great-grandfather Robert Todd (1697–1775) was also the great-great-great-grandfather of Mary Todd Lincoln.

PLACES TO VISIT

Battle of Corydon Memorial Park
565 Old Highway 135
Corydon, IN
(812) 738-8236
www.corydonbattlepark.com/battle.html

Blue River Church of Christ and Cemetery
Gravestone of Josiah Lincoln
11750 Fredericksburg Road Northwest
Depauw, IN

Christ Episcopal Church
506 Mulberry Street
Madison, IN
(812) 265-2158
cecmadison.org

Corydon Capitol State Historic Site
202 East Walnut Street
Corydon, IN
(812) 738-4890
https://www.indianamuseum.org/
corydon-capitol-state-historic-site

Emilie Todd Helm Home
610 West Main Street
Madison, IN
The Emilie Todd Helm home is privately owned and not open
to the public, but Main Street, which is lined with beautiful
historic homes, is perfect for a stroll.

Governor's House
Walnut Street
Corydon, IN
(812) 738-4890
https://www.indianamuseum.org

Jeremiah Sullivan Home
304 West Second Street
Madison, IN
(812) 265-2967
https://www.nps.gov/nr/travel/madison/judge_jeremiah
_sullivan_house.html

Jesse Bright Home

312 West Third Street

Madison, IN

https://www.nps.gov/nr/travel/madison/Jesse_Bright
_House.html

The home of Jesse Bright, Indiana's outspokenly pro-slavery
United States senator during the Civil War, is privately owned
and not open to the public, but the street, lined with beautiful
historic homes, is perfect for a stroll.

John Hunt Morgan Trail

https://www.hhhills.org/John-Hunt-Morgan.html

trailsrus.com/morgan

Kintner House

101 South Capitol Avenue

Corydon, IN 47112

(812) 738-2020

http://www.kintnerhouse.com

Lanier Mansion State Historic Site

601 West 1st Street

Madison, IN

(812) 265-3526

https://www.indianamuseum.org/lanier-mansion-and-state
-historic-site#about

Spring Mill State Park

3333 State Road 60 East

Mitchell, IN 47446

(812) 849-3534

https://www.in.gov/dnr/parklake/2968.htm

Squire Boone Caverns/Village

100 Squire Boone Road Southwest

Mauckport, IN

(812) 732-2782

https://www.squireboonecaverns.com

5

SOUTHWESTERN INDIANA

Life in Little Pigeon Creek

Interstate 64 cuts through sheer limestone cliffs and vast tracts of the Hoosier National Forest as it winds its way southwest from Corydon toward Abraham Lincoln's boyhood home in Lincoln City, a journey of about fifty-seven miles. If Thomas Lincoln and his family followed this route but stopped to visit relatives in Jasper (that's if they traveled by land), add another few miles to the journey. Of course, back in the day, that trip would have meant going up and down steep, rocky hills and following narrow pathways barely cleared by early settlers through almost impenetrable tracts of woods. Make the hour-plus trip more like a week, and it's easy to see why the Lincolns might have chosen to travel by river.

If the Lincolns started their trip on the Ohio River, they still would have faced a rough journey after landing on the Indiana riverbank. The family, which at that time included a cow and a dog as well as two horses carrying all their possessions, would then have had to trudge sixteen miles over forested ridges and deep hollows until they reached Little Pigeon Creek. Nancy and the children would have carried bundles and baskets, while Thomas would have led the horses and carried a gun as they made their way through the wilderness. Not exactly a fun-filled family trip.

No matter how they got there, this was a wild region, more so than Kentucky or Harrison County. But for the Lincolns, it was also a land of opportunity. By registering a claim at the land office in Vincennes, further west on the Wabash River, they would have time to pay off the property and fully own their farm. It was a straightforward deal, unlike their experiences in Kentucky. For a man with no money and no education but a willingness to work hard it was a chance to start over.

Abraham Lincoln was seven when his family settled in Little Pigeon Creek in December 1816. It was backwoods big time, and Lincoln, is said to have described it thus in a written autobiographical statement to Jesse W. Fell, December 20, 1859: "We reached our new home about the time the State came into the union. It was a region with many bears and other wild animals still in the woods. There I grew up."

LINCOLN BOYHOOD
NATIONAL MEMORIAL

The best place to start tracing Lincoln's path through southwest Indiana is the home where he lived from the ages of seven to twenty-one years. Though the original cabins are long gone, the two-hundred-acre Lincoln Boyhood National Memorial preserves the site of Thomas Lincoln's family farm. To get there means leaving the interstate and navigating a two-lane road as it makes a wide sweep down a wooded hill and through a dense copse of woods. I follow the road through Santa Claus—yes,

The Lincoln Boyhood National Memorial in Lincoln City, Indiana, honors the fourteen years that Lincoln and his family lived in this area between 1816 and 1830. Its visitor's center features a fifteen-minute video titled "Forging Greatness—Lincoln in Indiana" and a newly renovated museum. *Photo courtesy of Spencer County Visitors Bureau.*

there's really a town by that name and an old one as well, founded in 1856, but more about that later—and for brief moments, as the bucolic landscape flashes by, it's easy to feel you're driving through scenery from several hundred years ago. Horses graze in fields, and livestock nestle behind split-rail fences. The names of Lincoln's neighbors—Turnham, Gentry, Brooner—are stenciled on mailboxes and written up in the town census. Many of their ancestors were here when the Lincolns lived here and many of their families have remained.

"It's still a remote rural area," says Jim Hevron, whose family owns a cupboard carved by Tom Lincoln. Though the Hevron piece isn't on display, you can get an idea of Tom Lincoln's carpentry skills from the intricacies of similar cabinets of his in the Museum of Arts and Sciences in Evansville; at the Abraham Lincoln Presidential Library and Museum in Springfield, Illinois; and at the Indiana State Museum in Indianapolis. A

These sculpted limestone panels at the Lincoln Boyhood National Memorial in Spencer County, Indiana, depict major events in the life of Abraham Lincoln. *Photo courtesy of Spencer County Visitors Bureau*

desk built by Lincoln and traded for milling at Enlow's Mill in 1927 was given to the Lincoln Boyhood National Memorial and is on display there.

The entrance to the visitors' center at the Lincoln Boyhood National Memorial is flanked by five wonderfully sculpted limestone panels tracing the arc of the semicircular building. Created by sculptor E. H. Daniels, the panels portray scenes from Lincoln's life—his amazing rise from rustic boy to grand statesman who freed over four million people. Above the scenes, etched in stone, are nine inscriptions selected from Lincoln's writings showcasing his values and beliefs.

Inside, in cool halls sheltered from the weather by thick limestone walls (Indiana is, of course, known for its limestone, a lot of which went to build old New York), I peruse documents, examine artifacts, and watch a movie about Lincoln's life. I also stop to say hi to an old friend, Lincoln historian and author Mike Capps, chief of interpretation and resource management at the memorial, who has worked there for more than thirty years."Lincoln spent fourteen years living here, and this is where he grew up and became who he was," Capps often tells visitors, pointing out that Lincoln learned to work hard (though not necessarily like it) from his father. Indeed, Capps and I agree that though Kentucky and Illinois both claim him, Lincoln's formative years were very much shaped by the values, people, and living conditions of Indiana.

Nancy Hanks Lincoln's Untended Grave

Outside the visitor's center, past the tallest flagpole in the National Park Service, I follow the trail to the gravesite of Nancy Hanks Lincoln. A large marble headstone marks the spot—or very close to it, as the exact location isn't known. A fancy marker was way beyond the means of early pioneers like the Lincoln family, and after they left, the gravesite of the mother of one of the greatest US presidents was left untended and overgrown.

Protected now by an iron fence, Nancy's resting place engendered some controversy in 1868 when Civil War veteran William Q. Corbin saw the derelict condition of her grave and was moved to write a poem about it. The poem was published in the Rockport paper, which resulted in a two-foot marker being erected five years later, but by 1879 the marker had disappeared and the gravesite had become almost inaccessible because it was again so overgrown. Reading about the state of the gravesite of Lincoln's mother in 1874, Peter E. Studebaker, second vice president of the Studebaker Carriage Company, contacted Rockport postmaster L. S. Gilkey with instructions to buy the best tombstone available for fifty dollars and anonymously erect it on the site. Another fifty dollars, solicited from area residents, helped pay for the iron fence around the grave.

In his biography *Life of Lincoln*, William Herndon, Lincoln's third and last law partner, wrote of Nancy Hanks Lincoln,

> She was above the ordinary height in stature, weighed about 130 pounds, was slenderly built, and had much the appearance of one inclined to consumption. Her skin was dark; hair dark brown;

eyes gray and small; forehead prominent; face sharp and angular, with a marked expression for melancholy which fixed itself in the memory of all who ever saw or knew her. Though her life was clouded by a spirit of sadness, she was in disposition amiable and generally cheerful.

Maybe, just maybe, her look of melancholy came from being able to see far into the future, past the glory of her son becoming president and on to all the sorrow ahead. Or maybe it was from a hard life soon to come to an end.

Henry Brooner, who was Abraham Lincoln's childhood friend and whose mother died shortly before Nancy, and of the same illness, told Herndon about Nancy's burial: "I remember very distinctly that when Mrs. Lincoln's grave was filled, my father, Peter Brooner, extended his hand to Thomas Lincoln and said, 'We are brothers now', meaning that they were brothers in the same kind of sorrow. The bodies of my mother and Mrs. Lincoln were conveyed to their graves on sleds."

Lincoln Living Historical Farm

Nancy's quiet gravesite is near the spot where the family's cabin once stood, marked now by a bronze casting of cabin logs and a fireplace surrounded by a stone fence. Because they arrived so late in the year, Thomas was able to build only a three-sided lean-to. The following year, more family members arrived, including Nancy Hanks Lincoln's aunt and uncle, Thomas and Betsy Sparrow, and Dennis Hanks, who was the son of Nancy Lincoln's aunt Nancy. The Sparrows moved into the three-sided cabin, while the Lincolns and Dennis Hanks lived in the completed cabin Thomas had built when the weather warmed up.

Along a steep path, through fields of corn, wheat, and tall grasses, is the Living Historical Farm. Here park rangers dressed in period clothing perform the onerous, seemingly endless everyday chores of pioneer life at the Lincoln homestead amid a collection of time- and place-appropriate replicas of farm buildings—a twenty-two-by-sixteen-foot log cabin,

The Lincoln Living Historical Farm, a re-created pioneer homestead with a cabin, outbuildings, split rail fences, farm animals, vegetable and herb gardens, and field crops, represents a typical farmstead in this part of Indiana during the 1820s. Rangers in period clothing perform a variety of activities typical of that era. *Photo courtesy of Spencer County Visitors Bureau*

barn, smokehouse, carpenter shop, corncrib, and hen house. A costumed interpreter explains that back in Lincoln's time there would have been cows, horses, and sheep as well as the chickens that are running around. With the animals would have come plenty of opportunities for messy and smelly manure. Not trying to be gross here, just saying.

The inside of the cabin, though swept clean and made sweet smelling with fresh herbs and baking bread, seems way too small to have housed all the people who lived here. Did everyone get along on long, dark winter nights? And it's here, too, that Nancy Lincoln, in desperate pain, once lay dying. I think of what, in the days before disinfectants, Swiffers, and indoor plumbing, the ambience of the Lincoln home would have been like. Log cabin living two centuries ago seems less than romantic.

"Mother told me many times . . . about the first house Uncle Tom built when he came to Indiana," Dr. James LeGrand told Arthur Morgan, who was staying at the LeGrand Hotel the doctor and his wife owned in Jasper, Arkansas. LeGrand was the son of Sophie Hanks LeGrand, the illegitimate daughter of Nancy Hanks's sister, Sarah (Polly) Hanks. Sophie was among the many children and relatives who at various times lived in the Lincolns' cabin.

> It was a three-cornered house, made out of three rows of logs, with a fireplace in one corner. . . . He lived just through the winter in this shanty. In talking about it, he called it his "winter castle." How I come to know what kind of a house Abe Linkhorn lived in . . . mother an' I was coming from Jasper to Limestone Valley one night when we come to a little house this side of Limestone Valley, and she made me drive around it. She said it was just like the house Abe Linkhorn lived in. Uncle Tom built another house afterwards. (Arthur E. Morgan, "New Light on Lincoln's Boyhood," *Atlantic*, February 1920)

> Even the best of the log cabins for people like the Lincolns weren't in any way luxurious. In 1819, William Faux told Lincoln biographer Albert Beveridge the cabin belonging to John Ingle was the best he'd seen in southern Indiana. But here's what Faux meant by the best at that time: "Two men slept together next to 'six fine but dirty children,' while Mrs. Ingle and the hired girl slept in another bed. 'Males dress and undress before the females and nothing is thought of it. Shame or rather . . . false shame, or delicacy, does not exist here. It is not unusual for a male and a female to sleep in the same room uncurtained, holding conversations while in bed'" (Albert J. Beveridge, quoting William Faux, in *Abraham Lincoln, 1809–1858*, 51n2).

I'm thinking the description of "conversations" in the same "un-curtained" room really meant, well, maybe something more than just talking. After all, considering the number of babies being born, who really had much time to talk after a hard day's work?

MILLING AROUND LITTLE PIGEON CREEK

Enlow Mill: The Jasper City Mill

At one time, mills were the center of rural life, and from early pioneer beginnings well into the twentieth century, almost every settlement on a creek or river had at least one mill. Even now it's possible to retrace the roads that the Lincolns followed as they traveled to area mills. The seventeen miles from Little Pigeon Creek, now Lincoln City, to Enlow Mill, now the Jasper City Mill, on US 231 North is a short trip by automobile. But when Abe and his father took their oxen-pulled wagon loaded with grain over rutted dirt roads to the mill, the journey took so long they often spent the night with the Enlows.

The Enlows bought the mill in 1820 from Colonel Andrew Evans, a Revolutionary War veteran who built it around 1813. Over the years, the need for mills lessened, and Enlow Mill was abandoned and left derelict; what was left of it washed away in a flood during the 1960s. Almost half a century later, Ron Flick, an architect and preservationist whose family settled in Jasper in 1849, used the historic plans to recreate the Enlow's two-story mill, incorporating salvaged waterwheel parts from Virginia and the original two-hundred-year-old imported French millstones. Located on a river walk that follows the Patoka and connects the mill to a pretty park, the restored mill is open for tours and has a shop for buying ground flour and meal. It's a lovely spot with interesting connections to the Lincoln family. The Enlows were neighbors of the Lincolns in Kentucky, and Eleanor Enlow was said to have been the midwife at Abe Lincoln's birth. And, just to remind you, some say that Abe Lincoln's father was really a man with the last name of Enlow.

In Lincoln's time, the demand for grinding grains after the harvest sometimes meant long waiting lines, and visits to the mill were often social events, with men swapping stories, arguing about politics, and sipping White Dog or moonshine—rough whiskey. The latter was plentiful as mill owners often took a share of the grain to ferment their own booze. "No difference if grain was scarce or dear, or times hard, or the people poor, they would make and drink whiskey," William Cooper Howells wrote in *Recollections of Life in Ohio from 1813 to 1840*, and there's no reason to believe it wasn't true in any of the places Lincoln lived. "And the number of little distilleries was wonderful. Within two miles of where we lived there were three of them. . . . The custom was for every man to drink it, on all occasions that offered, and the women would take it sweetened and reduced to toddy" (125). In other words, people were semi-soused most of the time.

HUFFMAN'S MILL COVERED BRIDGE AND A RAID NEAR LITTLE PIGEON CREEK

On the trail from Corydon to Vincennes, the Huffmans, another Kentucky family migrating to Indiana, camped at a ford on Anderson Creek. Its pastoral beauty so impressed George Huffman that he and his wife, Nancy McDaniel Huffman, returned and built a home there around 1810 and, much later, a mill. But, like Kentucky, Indiana had its share of battles with Native Americans fighting to hold on to their land.

The Raid on the Meeks Family and the Atha Meeks Memorial

A year after the Huffmans settled in Indiana, Shawnee Indians under the leadership of Set-te-tah raided two cabins built by a settler named Atha (sometimes spelled Athe) Meeks and his family in nearby Little Pigeon Creek. Meeks's son, also named Atha, was the first to be shot by the Shawnees. Meeks, a Revolutionary War veteran, rushed to the aid of his son as they were attempting to scalp him but was fatally shot by Big Bones, another member of the raiding party. Meeks's wife managed to drag her husbands' body into their cabin but was struck by a tomahawk blow. Though wounded, Atha Jr. was able to fend off the attackers, giving his brother William time to shoot Big Bones. The remaining Shawnees fled, but some were captured and taken to the cabin of Justice of the Peace Uriah Lamar.

Or at least that's one story. When I interviewed Steve Sisley, a Spencer County historian, he said the body of Big Bones was found in a tree, and family tradition has it that the remaining Meekses used his skull as a drinking vessel. Hard times make folks hard, as shown further by what supposedly happened to Set-te-tah after he was captured during the fight. "Believing that one of the men wouldn't approve of killing Set-te-tah, they sent him to a well to get water, but he returned before the killing was accomplished. So one of the men spilled the water and they sent him out again," says Sisley. "When he returned Set-te-tah was dead."

It's a half-hour drive southwest from the site of the raid in Little Pigeon Creek to the Richland City area where Atha Meeks Jr. later lived and died, but it's there in the Graff Cemetery that a memorial to Atha Meeks tells the story of the family's settlement near Little Pigeon Creek and the fateful raid on their homestead:

> Pioneer and Revolutionary War veteran Athe Meeks Sr. (1750–1812) and his family settled near lake drain's entrance to Pigeon Creek in 1805. Seven years later at age 62 he was brutally killed on his doorstep and went down in history as the last white man murdered by the Indians in Indiana Territory. His 19-year-old son, Athe Jr. (1793–1843) was wounded during the encounter. Atha Sr. was buried in a field at the site of the tragedy near his cabin. Atha Jr., his wife Anna Vest Meeks (1797–1843), and several other family members are buried in this cemetery.

The cemetery and memorial are located south of Bullocktown off 900 West near County Road 500 in Spencer County.

The Huffman Mill and Covered Bridge

When the Huffmans heard the story about the attack on the Meeks family, they rethought their living arrangements and moved back to Kentucky. After fighting in the War of 1812, the

Spanning the Anderson River near where the old Huffman Mill once operated, the Huffman Bridge wasn't built until 1864. Still standing today near some of the foundations of the old mill, it marks where the Lincolns used to bring their grain. *Photo courtesy of Jane Simon Ammeson*

Huffmans rethought their decision again, and the couple, along with their infant son John, returned to Spencer County and built the water-powered Huffman Mill, which was both a saw-mill and gristmill.

Though the Huffman Mill is no longer standing, part of its old foundation can be seen while visiting the Huffman Mill Covered Bridge located on County Road 1490 North near St. Meinrad. You'll need a really good map for this one, but it's worth it. Spanning the Anderson River, the 148-foot wooden bridge wasn't built until 1864, but the setting hasn't changed that much since Lincoln and his childhood friend Henry Brooner would make the sixteen-mile trip by horseback to have their grain milled.

From an old advertising calendar:

George Huffman died in the year 1854 and the son, John Harrison Huffman, being the only child, succeeded to his father's estate and continued the pursuits of his father in milling, farming and stock raising until he accumulated a competency second to none in the county. He was married in the year 1840 to Delilah L. Stapleton, a native of Kentucky, and to them were born nine children, six of whom lived to their maturity. George W., the eldest, enlisted in the 49th Ind. Vol. and was killed at the siege of Vicksburg in 1863.

Prior to the Civil War John Harrison Huffman constructed a steam mill a short distance west of the water mill. This mill was burned in 1864 and he then reconstructed the dam and water mill which he and his son, L. Q. Huffman, operated until the year 1888, at which time the mill was taken over by his son John R. Huffman, and was operated by him until the year 1912, when it was sold and removed and the dam was destroyed.

This calendar is presented to you with the compliments of Benj. F. Huffman, son of L. Q. Huffman, and the great grandson of the pioneer, George Huffman.

LIFE IN LITTLE PIGEON CREEK

There were a few stores in the area, such as those owned by James Gentry, the Turnhams, and William Jones, but overall there was little to buy in the early years in Little Pigeon Creek. Though the area would later boom, becoming known as Lincoln City and boasting a railroad station, hotels, and businesses, that was in the future. In his interviews with the children of Nancy Hanks Lincoln's niece Sophie Hanks LeGrand, *Atlantic* correspondent Arthur E. Morgan was given a lesson in early pioneer economics by Sophie's son, Dr. LeGrand:

> Commerce, other than neighborhood barter, hardly existed in Thomas Lincoln's environment. The neighborhood was very nearly complete in itself, furnishing its own food, cloth, shoes, and farm-equipment. There being no market for corn, there was little incentive to raise more than could be used at home. This spirit still lingers in out-of-the-way places, where, in response to the question, "How much corn did you raise this year?" I frequently have received the answer, "We raised plenty of corn," or

Dressing in period clothes and doing chores that settlers two hundred years ago would have performed is part of the fun for those attending Spencer County's Fall Festival. *Photo courtesy of Spencer County Visitors Bureau*

"All the corn that we need." The doctor spoke of the gratification in the early days over an extra-large crop, its significance being that it would not be necessary to raise so much the following year. With little to buy, and with still less to sell, the environment seemed to furnish small stimulus to commercial ambition. (Arthur E. Morgan, "New Light on Lincoln's Boyhood")

Death was close and familiar to those living back then. According to Ancestry.com, by one estimate, a white man who had reached his twentieth birthday could expect to live just another nineteen years. A white woman at twenty would live, on average, an additional 18.8 years. If measuring from birth and counting infant mortality, life expectancy would have been even lower. A white family in the early nineteenth century would typically have seven or eight children, but one would die by age one and another before age twenty-one. And of course for slaves childhood deaths were higher and life expectancy even lower. About one in three young African American children died, and only half lived to adulthood.

Death had an early and lasting impact on Abraham and Mary Todd Lincoln, who both lost their mothers when they were young. Abe grew up hearing the story of how his grandfather Captain Abraham Lincoln was murdered by Indians. Tom and Nancy Lincoln's youngest child died at birth. Their only daughter, Sarah Lincoln Grigsby, and her infant son died during childbirth. Sarah Johnston, Lincoln's stepmother, was left a widow with three children. Life was short and seemingly unfair indeed.

For some reason, Nancy Hanks Lincoln is known as an angelic mother, while Thomas Lincoln is often disparaged as being a heavy whiskey consumer, unsophisticated, lazy, averse to his son's interest in learning, and harshly punitive. Not necessarily so according to Dr. LeGrand, a Lincoln relative. LeGrand told the story of how Thomas Lincoln lost a boatload of pork in the Patoka River to reporter Arthur E. Morgan, who wrote:

> The fact that Thomas Lincoln paid his debts after this experience, a labor which required several years, was repeatedly impressed upon me during my various visits with the doctor. The family traditions are colored throughout with a high regard for Thomas Lincoln's character, for his patience, kindness of heart, and honesty, and his finer sensibilities. Frequent reference was made to his consideration in disciplining his children. "Uncle Tom would not whip Abe or scold him before folk, but he would take him by himself and tend to him after they was gone. People in them days believed that whipping was good for children. Ma said she must have been pretty good, because she never got reproved or scolded very much." (Arthur E. Morgan, "New Light on Lincoln's Boyhood")

Thomas might have at times been harsh, and Lincoln may have resented how his father treated him. But there are upper-middle-class children today who feel resentful of their parents because they don't get what they want. In Tom's defense, he never deserted his family, was never said to be unfaithful, and tried to provide for them. When choosing a second wife, he made an extremely wise decision in marrying Sarah Johnston, a widow with three children of her own who immediately stepped into the role of motherhood, cleaned up the Lincoln cabin, and gave love and guidance to the Lincoln children. He also appeared to be a good husband, taking in Nancy's aunt and uncle, Elizabeth and Thomas Sparrow, Nancy's niece Sophie Hanks, and Dennis Hanks, the illegitimate son of Nancy Hanks, an aunt of Lincoln's mother, also named Nancy Hanks. It does get confusing, doesn't it?

Jim Hevron, whose family came to southwest Indiana a few years after the Lincolns and who is related to many of Tom and Nancy's neighbors, including the Romines and the Gentrys, says he doesn't believe the relationship between Tom and Abraham was as testy as many described. "If it was that bad why would he have moved with his father to Illinois?" he says. "And people made much of the fact that he didn't go to his father's funeral. But it was the middle of winter and it would have taken days by horse to get through all the snow to attend the funeral. He might not have even known about it until after it was over."

It's possible that Thomas was just trying to steer his son in the right direction and believed that a man succeeded not by schooling but through muscle and strength. When talking to Lincoln biographer William Herndon, William Green recounted the heated disagreements between father and son over Abe wasting his time reading. Green recalled Thomas talking about his son five years after he'd moved out of the family home at age twenty-two.

"I suppose that Abe is still fooling hisself with eddication. I tried to stop it, but he had got that fool idea in his head, and it can't be got out. Now I hain't got no eddication, but I get along far better than ef I had . . . if Abe don't fool away all his time on his books, he may make something yet."

LINCOLN STATE PARK

Just across the street from the Lincoln Boyhood National Memorial, the 1,747-acre Lincoln State Park was established in 1932 as a memorial to Nancy Hanks Lincoln. The state park's amenities include the Lincoln Amphitheatre, the only completely covered amphitheater in the United States, which presents dramatizations of Lincoln's life as well as other plays and music. The park also provides boat rentals, a nature center, and hiking trails. But the most unique attractions are the many remnants of the Lincolns' life in the park.

Little Pigeon Church and Cemetery

Tom Lincoln helped build Little Pigeon Church in 1821, making the window frames, door casings, and pulpit. The first Little Pigeon Church (there would be a second built in 1875 and the present one in 1948) was twenty-six by thirty feet and built of hewn logs. The fireplace and chimney were of brick made by David Turnham; the mold was fashioned by Tom using wooden pegs and no iron. A piece of stone from the original foundation remains with the church that is standing on the site today.

Sarah Lincoln Grigsby, Abe's older sister, was just twenty-one when she died on January 20, 1828. She was buried with her child in her arms in the Little Pigeon Baptist Church cemetery, also in the park. Sarah's husband, Aaron, is buried nearby. He remarried in 1830, had a daughter with his new wife, and then died the following year at age thirty. He left a considerable estate for that time and area—worth around $300—that included geese, hogs, chickens, and a horse.

Born in 1808 in Elizabethtown, Kentucky, Sarah was nine when the family moved to Indiana. Two years later, on October 5, 1818, her mother Nancy would die of what was known as milk sickness because it came from the milk of cows who had ingested white snakeroot, a poisonous weed. Nancy had spent her last days nursing her neighbor Allen Brooner's mother, who also died of the disease. About that time Nancy's aunt and uncle, the Sparrows, who were living in the first cabin Tom built on the Lincoln homestead, also passed away from milk sickness.

Before Tom Lincoln remarried, Sarah helped care for her younger brother and also took on most of the household duties. She attended school sporadically, as did her brother, but probably somewhat more than many pioneer girls did in Indiana at that time.

One of Sarah's duties when her mother died was performing burial preparations—washing, dressing, and placing her body in the casket that her father and brother had made. Nancy was buried on the rise of a hill that overlooked the farm where the family lived. Sarah wouldn't live that much longer herself. Shortly after joining the Little Pigeon Baptist Church on April 8, 1826, Sarah married Aaron Grigsby on August 2 of that year and moved to a cabin about two miles from her family. Nine months after their marriage, the couple announced Sarah was pregnant. She would die of unknown complications during labor.

On the night Sarah passed away, Abe was at Reuben Grigsby Sr.'s house. Reuben's son Redmond Grigsby remembered later that "Abe was out in our little smoke house doing a little carpenter work, when Aaron, Sarah's husband, came running up from his house a quarter-mile away and said that Sarah had just died."

"I never will forget that scene," Grigsby said. "Abe sat down in the door of the smoke house and buried his face in his hands. The tears slowly trickled from between his bony fingers and his gaunt frame shook with sobs." Mrs. J. W. Lamar, a neighbor of the Grigsbys, also recalled the night Sarah died. "My mother was there at the time. She [Sarah] had a strong voice, and I heard her calling her father. He went after a doctor but it was too late. They let her lay too long."

Whether Sarah was calling for her father as she lay dying and whether a doctor could have saved her isn't known, as medical training back then was somewhat sporadic and there were no doctors nearby. But Abe Lincoln, who was extremely close to his sister—she was credited with helping him learn his numbers and letters—blamed Aaron Grigsby for her death, accusing him of neglect. Though the Lincolns and the Grigsbys had been close, both coming from Kentucky, settling near each other in Little Pigeon Creek, and attending the same church, the two families became estranged.

Lincoln's anger toward the Grigsbys lasted until 1844 when, while speaking to an audience in his campaign for Henry Clay, he spotted one of Aaron's brothers in the group and called out to him, asking to meet afterward. In 1860, when Lincoln was running for the presidency, Nathaniel, who was nicknamed Natty and was living in Missouri by then, wrote to him asking to be named as Republican Precinct Committee man. He placed Lincoln's name on the ballot there in 1860 and soon learned that it wasn't a popular move among his neighbors, who were Southern sympathizers. A friendlier neighbor rode up to his house around two or three in the morning and warned him not to light any lights, as his neighbors were planning to murder him. If he wanted to live, Natty should be on his way. Taking the warning seriously, Natty moved back to Spencer County, where he and four of his five sons joined Company C, Tenth Indiana Cavalry, and he was named second lieutenant. Nathaniel would have a much longer life than Sarah, her babe, Aaron, or Abe, living until 1890.

Gordon's Mill: A Kick to the Head

The sites of Noah Gordon's mill and homestead are also part of Lincoln State Park. Gordon, a neighbor of the Lincoln family, owned a small grain mill where Lincoln was "killed for a while" one day after being kicked in the head by his horse while milling grain. Powered by horses rather than water, Gordon's Mill was a slow-moving mill, and it took a lot of time to grind grain. Lincoln, who had walked the two miles from his cabin, was impatient as he waited his turn and the sun began to set.

Watching the horses slowly go round and round, young Lincoln commented that "his dog could eat the meal as fast as the mill could grind it." Eventually it was Abraham's turn, and he hitched his old mare to the gristmill's arm. To keep the horse moving, he hit it with a whiplash, clucked in the normal manner, and shouted, "Git up, you old hussy; git up, you old hussy." Just as he yelled the words "Git up" again, the horse kicked backward with a hind foot, hitting him in the head. Lincoln was knocked down and out. Noah Gordon ran to his aid and picked up the bleeding, unconscious lad. Dave Turnham, who had come to the mill with Abraham, ran to get Abraham's father. Thomas Lincoln hauled his injured son home in a wagon and put him to bed. He lay unconscious all night.

Apparently, some (including Noah Gordon) thought he was dead or near death. Neighbors flocked to the Lincolns' cabin. The next morning an onlooker cried, "He's coming straight back from the dead!" Abraham jerked all over. Suddenly he blurted out the words "You old hussy," thus finishing what he was about to say before the horse knocked him out. In discussing the affair, Lincoln himself used the words "apparently killed for a time."

The Andrew Crawford School

The first school Abraham and Sarah Lincoln attended in Indiana stood east of the Little Pigeon Church and cemetery on Noah Gordon's land, now at an uncertain location on the grounds of Lincoln State Park. A one-room hewn-log building sixteen feet wide by twenty-six feet long, Crawford's School had a greased-paper window, a puncheon floor, and split-log benches. Pegged to the wall above the door was a fine pair of buck antlers. Abe and Sarah's teacher was Andrew Crawford, who, according to Nathaniel Grigsby, taught good manners and "the three Rs." It was considered a blab school, the name given to early settler schools where students recited or blabbed their lessons out loud, separately or in chorus with others, as a way of learning. Eleven-year-old Abe Lincoln helped Ann Roby spell the word "defied" by pointing to his own eye during a spelling contest. But helping pretty Ann spell the word correctly didn't win her heart. Though Lincoln was said to have had a mash (crush) on her, Ann married Allen Gentry, one of Abe's good friends.

Lincoln would go on to have other short-lived romances as well. According to J. Edward Murr in his 1918 article "Lincoln in Indiana" for the *Indiana Magazine of History,* William Richardson moved with his family, including his daughter Polly, to southwestern Indiana. Unloading some of their possessions after crossing the Ohio River, they made their way to a cluster of trees where they could make a lean-to or house by cutting brush and placing it against poles. This would be their new home for a while until something more permanent could be built. The men then left Polly and her mother while they returned to the river to get more of the family's belongings.

By nightfall and with a storm approaching, the women became worried that something had happened to the men. Their anxieties weren't in the least alleviated when a tall stranger appeared carrying a gun and wearing a coonskin hat, a hunting shirt, and buckskin breeches. He was there, he told them, because he lived a short distance away and had heard that a new family was moving into the community. He had come to see if he could help. When Mrs. Richardson said that her "men folk" had gone back to the river to get another load of their belongings and would be back soon, the stranger responded, "Well, ladies, I'm quite sure they cannot get back tonight, for the rain has interfered, and so I'll just stay with you and see that no harm comes to you during the night."

As one could imagine, this was not entirely reassuring. They watched as this very tall man seated himself beneath a tree near their brush hut, put the rifle across his lap, and leaned against the trunk, indicating that he was there to stay.

Polly's recollections were reported years later by J. Edward Murr:

> Seeing this, Mrs. Richardson stepped into the brush house and she and the daughter held a whispered consultation. It was agreed that while the stranger might prove to be more dangerous than any foe of the woods, yet the mother suggested that "he had a good face." After a few moments in conversation they observed that the stranger had laid down his gun and began

dragging a large limb toward the brush house. The mother and daughter both ventured out near him and requested to know what he meant by such procedure.

Whereupon he smiled and said: "Ladies, the woods around here are full of wolves and bears, and we've got to have a bonfire tonight or they might give trouble." When the mother remarked that they entertained no fear of wolves, the man laughed right heartily and said: "You just wait and we'll see if there isn't about two women around here somewhere that'll get pretty badly scared before long." With that remark, he began the search for dry branches and limbs of fallen trees and this he continued doing until there was collected quite a pile.

When darkness had settled down over them and the wagon had not returned as the stranger had ventured to prophesy, the ladies became more or less reconciled to the presence of the man. He accepted the food they prepared, but refused to go into the lean-to. An hour or so had passed, when the stranger, who all this time was watched from within with some remaining suspicion, called to them that they need have no fears of wolves who by this time were howling in the distance. Ere long these denizens of the night ventured quite near, and the ladies, thoroughly frightened, requested that he come into the lean-to. The stranger then approached the bonfire and requested Mrs. Richardson and her daughter to "step out and take a look at the green-eyes." This they did, and the daughter exclaimed in her fright: "Why, mother, there is a thousand of them. What would we have done alone?" The tall stranger laughed and said, addressing the young lady: "Miss, there is not more than a half dozen of the varmints, and every one of them is a coward. Now you just see if they are not." Taking a fire brand and waving it vigorously, the "green eyes" vanished and the howling was heard in the distance. The manifest danger confronting the ladies by the presence of such animals drew them nearer to their protector, and they acted on his suggestion to "go in and try and get some sleep while he kept watch." When morning broke the stranger announced his intention of returning home, saying as he started: "I'll find out today if your men folks get back all right, which I reckon they will, but if they don't, I'll be back here tonight and we'll keep the 'thousand pairs of green eyes' at a safe distance." (Murr, "Lincoln in Indiana," 54-55)

Of course, we don't really need to tell you that the tall stranger with the coonskin cap was the future president, do we?

Lincoln became friendly with Polly Richardson, taking her to spelling bees, play parties, and church. He impressed her father with his strength when he picked up a chicken coop that William Richardson and several friends were getting ready to move and carried it all by himself for some distance. Richardson estimated the chicken house "weighed at least six hundred pounds, and maybe more."

As for Polly, she claimed she was Lincoln's first sweetheart. If she had known, she later said, that he would become president, she would have accepted his proposal of marriage.

The Gentry Store

The Romine-Hevron-Gentry families, who migrated to Little Pigeon Creek after the Lincolns, owned vast tracts of property in Lincoln City and Gentryville. The Romine-Hevron farm remained in the family for four generations until the land was acquired by the expanding state and national parks. "Our ancestors deeded the church and cemetery where Sarah Lincoln and her child are buried," says Jim Hevron, noting that James and Elizabeth Gentry came to the Little Pigeon Creek area in the early 1800s, as did Christopher and Margaret Romine.

There was a short-lived romance between James and Elizabeth's daughter Hannah Gentry and Lincoln, which ended for a rather odd reason: "Abraham Lincoln and Hannah Gentry were a twosome for a while but Abe had a fondness for green onions and Hannah said that she was not going to get near anyone who smelled of an onion patch. We wonder how differently the family history might have read if Abraham Lincoln and Hannah Gentry had decided to marry." (*Our Lincoln Heritage: The Hevron Family Cookbook: One Hundred Seventy-Five Years for Recipes and Reflections*). Hannah Gentry instead married Christopher and Margaret's son John Romine on April 5, 1829.

James Gentry, who owned around 5000 acres of land, was considered one of the richest men around. Lincoln never seemed

During his youth in Little Pigeon Creek Lincoln worked for William Jones, who owned a store across the road from his home, now a state historic site open for visitors. Lincoln also spent the night at the home of William Jones when he returned to Indiana in 1844 to campaign for Henry Clay for president. *Photo courtesy of Spencer County Visitors Bureau*

to resent the success of others and instead enjoyed learning from them, often entering into mentoring relationships founded on friendship and knowledge. He worked for Gentry at one of his stores, the site of which is located off Trail 3 at Lincoln State Park. It was at Gentry's store, according to Dr. LeGrand, that Lincoln first sipped a cup of coffee, which back then in southwestern Indiana was very rare indeed.

> During the summer months, Abraham Lincoln spent much of his time clerking at Great-great-great Grandfather James Gentry's store. One afternoon he realized that he had short changed a customer by three cents. Just as soon as the store closed that evening, he walked two miles to be sure that the customer received the money that was due. (*Our Lincoln Heritage: The Hevron Family Cookbook*)

Colonel William Jones State Historic Site, Gentryville

Lincoln State Park also operates the Colonel William Jones State Historic Site, a ten minute drive west of the park in Gentryville, which is named after James Gentry. As a young man Lincoln worked for Jones, a successful merchant, and he would return to stay with Jones on his last trip to Indiana. As an old man, Jones would visit the newly elected President Lincoln in Springfield, Illinois. Restored in 1976, Jones's 1834 Federal brick home features a second-floor observatory and eleven-foot-high built-in cupboards beside the fireplace. Located on one hundred acres of forest, the property also includes a restored log barn.

THE DAVID TURNHAM HISTORICAL MARKER, LINCOLN CITY

The Turnhams and Lincolns had been friends when they lived in Kentucky, and after both families moved to southern Indiana, they became neighbors and friends once again. David Turnham (1803–1884), a prosperous farmer and justice of the peace, let Lincoln borrow *The Revised Laws of Indiana*, a five-hundred-page tome that contained the Declaration of Independence, the Constitution, the first twelve amendments, the Virginia Act of cession of the Northwest Territory, the Ordinance of 1787, the act admitting Indiana as a state, and the first state constitution. Lincoln read the book avidly and repeatedly. It certainly wasn't typical reading material for most kids of Lincoln's day—or even our own. Many couldn't read, and those who could probably wouldn't have chosen a book like this. There were no public schools yet, and families had to pay for their kids to attend the few private schools around. But being a voracious reader with unusual reading choices wasn't the only difference between Lincoln and many other kids.

"He loved fishing & hunted Some—not a great deal," Turnham would later say in an interview with Herndon reproduced by Douglas Wilson and Rodney Davis in *Herndon's*

Informants, adding that Lincoln was "naturally Cheerful and good natured while in Indiana." Other contemporaries would also recall that Lincoln didn't like killing animals. Of course, at that time, hunting was not a sport but a necessity in terms of putting meat on the table.

"Although quick witted and ready with an answer," David Turnham told Herndon, "he began to exhibit deep thoughtfulness and was so often lost in studied reflection we could not help noticing the strange sensitiveness, especially in the presence of men and women, and although cheerful enough in the presence of boys, he did not appear to seek our company as earnestly as before."

Driving east from Lincoln City on State Road 162 toward Santa Claus, you'll come across an Indiana Historical Marker in front of Heritage Hills High School at the intersection of SR 162 and CR 1600 North commemorating the Turnhams. It reads, in part: "In 1819, the Turnham family settled less than one-mile northeast of Thomas Lincoln's farm. . . . Turnham loaned Lincoln *Revised Laws of Indiana* (1824) in 1827. After Lincoln's assassination, he provided information to historians about Lincoln's youth." Turnham's copy of the book is now held at the Lilly Library at Indiana University Bloomington.

Next to Heritage Hills High School is Hoosier Land Pizza & Wings and a log cabin where Lincoln stayed in 1830 on his way to the Huffman Mill. Located on the long buffalo run where vast herds once made their way between the Wabash and Ohio Rivers, the property is on a parcel of land where Lincoln's cousin Dennis Hanks once lived.

O. V. BROWN–HOLIDAY WORLD LINCOLN COLLECTION, SANTA CLAUS

It's four miles east from Lincoln City on CR 162 to Santa Claus, home to Holiday World & Splashin' Safari, named by *USA Today* as the best water park in the nation. Holiday World is also well known for its award-winning wooden roller coasters, but what make it truly unique is that it may be the only theme park in the world where Abraham Lincoln's signature is on permanent display. O. V. Brown, a local historian with a passion for preserving Lincoln's heritage, donated the multitude of Lincoln artifacts he'd spent most of his life gathering, many from the president's fourteen years in Indiana, and they're all on display in the O. V. Brown–Holiday World Lincoln Collection. The exhibit consists of seventeen display cases filled with books, tools, letters, and clothing commemorating Lincoln's life and work.

The park's Lincoln Classroom exhibit includes such rare relics as a sample of Lincoln's handwriting dating back to his days as a young student; the earliest known published image of Abraham Lincoln; several presidential signatures; a cordial case owned by the Lincolns and used for entertaining at the White House; a mourning card acknowledging President Lincoln's death with mourning ribbon and Lincoln's photograph; and the ceremonial pen used by President Kennedy to sign the bill creating the Lincoln Boyhood National Memorial in Lincoln City.

ROCKPORT

The fastest way to Rockport from Santa Claus or Lincoln City is south from SR 162 on US 231, but I don't mind adding extra time to the trip by heading west and south toward Gentryville on SR 62 and journeying on the back roads through such small villages as Chisney, back east toward Grandview, and then down scenic SR 66 along the Ohio River. Rockport is a quaint river town with an old courthouse commanding the town square. Historic mansions line the bluff above the river, and the city has a Carnegie library, several nice shops, and numerous Lincoln connections.

Lincoln Landing

In 1828, Abraham Lincoln and Allen Gentry launched a flatboat filled with produce from a landing on River Road at the east

An Abraham Lincoln reenactor stands in front of the Lincoln
Pioneer Village and Museum in Rockport, Indiana. The village helps
visitors visualize what life in southwest Indiana was like when Lincoln
and his family lived here in the early 1800s. *Photo courtesy of
Spencer County Visitors Bureau*

end of Main Street in Rockport. Their journey took them to
New Orleans to sell goods from James Gentry's store. Besides
being an adventure for the nineteen-year-old Lincoln, the trip
was also a life changer: it was the first time he encountered the
horrors of slave auctions, experiences credited with forming
his strong antislavery beliefs. A stop on the Tri-State Heritage
Trail marks the Lincoln Flatboat Landing on First Street (also
known as River Road), a narrow road beneath the high bluff
where Rockport is perched.

From a young age Lincoln immersed himself in learning,
much to the disdain of his father and even some neighbors such
as James Gentry, who described him as lazy and always wanting to read. But he wasn't lazy when it came to learning law.
Lincoln would walk great distances to listen to court cases. He
often visited Rockport, where he became acquainted with John
Pitcher, the first resident attorney there, who afterward became

prosecuting attorney for Spencer County. Pitcher let Abe read the books in his library, including his law books. "He either had to walk or go by horseback," says Mike Capps about the seventeen-mile journey from Little Pigeon to Rockport. "But Lincoln had an inquisitive mind and he liked to be out and about."

The Lincoln Pioneer Village & Museum in Rockport features hundreds of artifacts from the area's past, including a hutch made by Tom Lincoln, who was, says Jim Hevron, an excellent carpenter. The Pioneer Village comprises thirteen cabins that are replicas from the Lincoln era, such as the Pioneer Schoolhouse, Lincoln Homestead Cabin, and Old Pigeon Baptist Church. Built as part of a WPA project, the village is the brainchild of George Honig, a Lincoln historian and sculptor, to create a visitor's visual experience of life in Lincoln's time.

The Squire Samuel Pate House

Lincoln's Ohio River trip led to the beginning of a career in law and politics and another fleeting romance.

Abraham Lincoln worked on a ferryboat near Posey's Landing on the Ohio River in Spencer County, Indiana, in the fall and winter of 1826–27. The following spring, Lincoln built a small flatboat for his own use at Bates' Landing about a mile and a half downriver. He intended to earn money by carrying produce down the river.

This business languished, however, and Lincoln, his meager savings gone, turned to carrying passengers to steamboats in the middle of the river. One day he was motioned to the Kentucky shore by John T. Dill and his brother who were operating a ferryboat nearby. A tense confrontation occurred as the brothers accused Lincoln of infringing on their business. Lincoln's obvious strength may have encouraged a legal rather than a physical resolution; in any event, Lincoln and the brothers turned to Samuel Pate, a farmer and justice of the peace.

The Dill brothers accused Lincoln of interfering with their legally established business. Lincoln admitted to conveying passengers to the middle of the river, but he argued that he had carried no one who was a potential customer of the Dills' ferry.

Lincoln ran a ferry across a section of the Ohio River much like this one below the tall bluffs of Rockport, the Spencer County seat.
Photo courtesy of Spencer County Visitors Bureau

Samuel Pate decided the case for Lincoln by narrowly interpreting the act from William Littell's Statute Law of Kentucky "respecting the Establishment of Ferries." The law prohibited unauthorized persons from carrying passengers "over" the river. Lincoln, however, had taken them only to the middle of the river.

This case, the first in which Lincoln appeared as a defendant, led to a friendship between him and Samuel Pate which, some have speculated, may have stimulated his initial interest in the law. (Kentucky Historical Society, "Kentucky's Abraham Lincoln: Abraham Lincoln Pleads His Own Case")

According to Spencer County historian Steve Sisley, folklore has it that while in the Pate home, Lincoln noticed Squire Pate's books and made several trips to the home to read them.

Not only did Lincoln win his first law case thanks to Judge Pate, but Pate had a niece named Caroline Meeker who sat in on the trial. She congratulated Lincoln when he won, and for the next few weeks, they spent time together. But the Meekers were a well-to-do, successful family, and, despite Lincoln's lawsuit, they didn't see any future in the poor ferryman and insisted Caroline discontinue the relationship. And so she did.

Little did they know.

Though it's in Kentucky, the Squire Samuel Pate House, built in 1822, is an important part of Lincoln's Indiana life and is now open to visitors. To get there, take US 231 south to the William Natcher Bridge and take US 60 east to Kentucky 334. The Pate home is on KY 334 near Lewisport. Lincoln Ferry Park, located at the point on Indiana Highway 66 where the Anderson River flows into the Ohio, not only marks the site where the Lincolns crossed the river on their journey to their new home but is also where Lincoln operated his ferryboat service.

ABRAHAM LINCOLN HISTORICAL MARKER, BOONVILLE

If you want to take a detour from Rockport back up to Gentryville and follow CR 62 to Boonville, you'll find a plaque in dedication to Abraham Lincoln on the northeast corner of the Warrick County courthouse that reads "While living with his father on a farm about seventeen miles from here came often to Boonville to hear court trials and to borrow books from John A. Brackenridge. From this corner Abraham Lincoln traveled north by ox-team on the old Boonville-Petersburg-Vincennes road when emigrating to Illinois in 1830. Sponsored by The Warrick County Historical Society, 1932." The payoff for Lincoln traveling the roughly twenty miles to Boonville, besides listening to Brackenridge argue cases, was the use of his library, which contained 457 books.

LEAVING INDIANA

"When the Lincolns were getting ready to leave," Allen Brooner told William Herndon in 1865 when the historian was collecting

The Warrick County Courthouse in Boonville, Indiana, was one of several courthouses where Lincoln would visit to listen to legal proceedings and borrow books from the county prosecutors.
Photo courtesy of Jane Simon Ammeson

information about Lincoln's time in Indiana, "Abraham and his stepbrother, John Johnston, came over to our house to swap a horse for a yoke of oxen. Abe was always a quiet fellow. John did all the talking and seemed to be the smartest of the two. If anyone had been asked that day which would make the greatest success in life, I think the answer would have been John Johnston" (Ida M. Tarbell, "Abraham Lincoln: A Life," 4).

John Johnston, the son of Lincoln's stepmother Sarah Johnston Lincoln, was a charming fellow who never amounted to much. He would often ask Lincoln for money.

> Your request for eighty dollars I do not think it best to comply with now," Lincoln wrote him back after one too many times of being hit up for money. "At the various times when I have helped you a little, you have said to me 'We can get along very well now;' but in a very short time I find you in the same difficulty again. Now this can only happen by some defect in your conduct. What that defect is I think I know. You are not lazy, and still you are an idler. (Abraham Lincoln, "Letter to John D. Johnston, January 2 [?], 1851," 144)

Johnston would also later remark, somewhat ruefully, that he too found it surprising that Lincoln had done so well and he not at all.

VINCENNES: MONUMENTS TO LINCOLN AND WILLIAM HENRY HARRISON

On March 1, 1830, the Lincolns stayed at the Gentry home before traveling to Vincennes, which had been the territorial capital. There the Lincoln family would spend several days resting and sightseeing while their wagon wheels were being repaired. Abe Lincoln, a regular reader of the Vincennes's *Western Sun* newspaper, is said to have visited the paper's offices. The printing press for the *Western Sun* is now at the Vincennes

It's said that Lincoln, an avid reader of newspapers, visited the print house for the *Western Sun* in Vincennes as his family traveled from Indiana to Illinois. *Photo courtesy of Jane Simon Ammeson*

State Historical Site, just a few blocks from Grouseland, the grand 1804 Georgian/Federal-style home of another president, William Henry Harrison, who lived in Vincennes while serving as governor of the Northwest Territory. Harrison's tenure as president was even shorter than Lincoln's, lasting only thirty-one days before he died of pneumonia.

While waylaid in Vincennes, the Lincolns would themselves visit Grouseland and also Vincennes's brand new cathedral. No longer new, it is now called the Old Cathedral Library and is open for tours, as is Grouseland. After three days in Vincennes, their wagon fixed, the Lincoln family would cross the Wabash into Illinois on what is now the Lincoln Memorial Bridge, US 50 Business. A statue of Lincoln as a young man commemorates the spot.

BACK HOME IN INDIANA

When Abraham Lincoln supped at the Noon Day Inn on October 31, 1844, the stagecoach stop in Warrenton had already been serving travelers for almost two decades. Still in business, it is the oldest restaurant in continuous operation in Indiana. Now expanded many times over, the interior and its original hewn log walls and chinking still remain much as they were when Lincoln came to dine.

Lincoln had returned to southwest Indiana for the first time since moving to Illinois a quarter century before. He was campaigning for Henry Clay, a man he had long admired, who was again running for president. Lincoln gave speeches promoting Clay's candidacy in Bruceville, Vincennes, Washington, Boonville, and other towns and cities in southern Indiana. He spoke in Rockport, standing in front of the county seat, and the next day he stopped at what is now the Log Inn, one of the main stagecoach stops on the road between Evansville and Vincennes, Indiana. The first stagecoach began making the run between Evansville and Vincennes in 1824, about a year before the Noon Day Inn (as it was called back then) opened.

Today you can make the twenty-five miles from Vincennes to Princeton in thirty minutes. The drive from Princeton to Evansville is slightly longer. Traveling by car, the twenty-nine-mile trip now takes just under forty minutes. Still, the entire journey is just over an hour. The entire trip back in Lincoln's day was twenty-one hours if the weather was good. That included the time it took for drivers to change horses. During the stopover, travelers could dine at the inn, which was built in 1825. In another connection to Lincoln, underneath what they now call the Lincoln Room is a crude basement that served as a stop on the Underground Railroad before and during the Civil War.

On this trip back to Indiana, Lincoln spent the night at the home of William Jones, visited his mother's grave, and spoke at a "Cross-road voting place" that he mentions in a letter to

Table 5.1. Evansville to Vincennes Stage Coach Schedule circa 1844[*]

Southbound Schedule		Northbound Schedule	
Vincennes Out	8:00 a.m. Wed.	Evansville Out	8:00 a.m. Sat.
Princeton In	5:00 p.m. Wed.	Princeton In	5:00 p.m. Sat.
Princeton Out	5:00 a.m. Thurs.	Princeton Out	8:00 a.m. Sun.
Evansville In		Vincennes In	5:00 p.m. Sun.

*Schedule based on good weather

Turnham. Jones, who served as a Whig representative in the Indiana legislature from 1838 to 1841, had hired Lincoln to do odd jobs in his youth, had him work as a clerk in his store, and let him read all his books. He supposedly remarked that "Lincoln would make a great man one of these days."

His perceptions were spot-on. Jones visited Lincoln after he was elected but before he left for Washington, DC. "Mr. Lincoln was called upon to-day by an old man from Indiana named Jones for whom thirty years ago he worked as a common farm-hand at a dollar a day," writes Jesse William Weik in his book *The Real Lincoln: A Portrait*. Though he was in his sixties, Jones was such an avid believer in the antislavery cause that he joined the Union Army at the outbreak of the Civil War and was serving as a lieutenant colonel of the Fifty-Third Regiment of Indiana Volunteers when he was killed at the Battle of Atlanta in 1864.

Long after he left Indiana, Lincoln often recalled his years there. A poem he wrote tells about the time when Little Pigeon Creek was a wilderness.

> When first my father settled here,
> Twas then the frontier line:
> The panthers scream, filled night with fear
> And bears preyed upon the swine.

Before he won the presidency, he also wrote to David Turnham, who he had seen on his visit there in 1844.

I well remember when you and I last met, after a separation of fourteen years, at the cross-road voting place, in the fall of 1844. It is now sixteen years more and we are both no longer young men. I suppose you are a grandfather; and I, though married much later in life, have a son nearly grown.

HISTORIC MANSIONS IN CRAWFORDSVILLE

If you're up for a side trip, consider visiting the Henry S. Lane House in Crawfordsville in west central Indiana. Lane, a founder of the Republican Party, an Indiana governor, a congressman, and a US senator, was a close friend of Abraham Lincoln. Lane chaired Lincoln's second inaugural committee and accompanied Lincoln's body to Springfield for burial. Though Lincoln never visited the beautiful Greek Revival Lane mansion, with its columned porches and manicured lawn, the house is one of the few museums where 95 to 98 percent of everything in the house is original, including mementos of Lane's deep friendship with Lincoln. These include the black silk hat Lane wore to his friend's funeral, which still hangs on the hall tree, Lincoln's autograph on a calling card, a wreath from his coffin, and the black badge Lane wore when he served as pallbearer. A lock of the president's hair, taken after he died, is also on display.

Just a few blocks away is the General Lew Wallace Study. Wallace, the youngest major general in the Union army, was Lane's brother-in-law and the author of the best-selling book *Ben-Hur*. After Lincoln's death, Wallace was appointed to the military commission in charge of the trial of the conspirators in the Lincoln assassination.

PLACES TO VISIT

West Central Indiana Destinations

Lane Place
212 South Water Street
Crawfordsville, IN
(765) 362-3416
http://www.lane-mchs.org/

General Lew Wallace Study and Museum
200 Wallace Avenue
Crawfordsville, IN
(765) 362-5769
https://www.ben-hur.com/

Southwest Indiana Destinations

Colonel William Jones State Historic Site
620 East County Road 1575 North
Gentryville, IN
(812) 937-4710

Enlow Mill / Jasper City Mill
100, 164 3rd Avenue
(812) 482-4924

Grouseland
3 West Scott Street
Vincennes, IN
(812) 882-2096
http://www.grouselandfoundation.org/

Heritage Hills High School
SR 162 and CR 1600 North
Lincoln City, IN

Holiday World & Splashin' Safari
452 East Christmas Boulevard
Santa Claus, IN
(812) 937-4401
https://www.holidayworld.com/

Hoosier Land Pizza & Wings
3804 IN-162
Lincoln City, IN
(812) 937-2799
https://www.facebook.com/HoosierLandPizza/

Huffman Mill Covered Bridge
County Road 1490 North
St. Meinrad, IN

Lincoln Boyhood National Memorial
3027 East South Street
Lincoln City, IN
(812) 937-4541
https://nps.gov/libo/index.htm

Lincoln Ferry Park
12789 IN-66
Troy, IN
http://santaclausind.org/listings/lincoln-ferry-park

Lincoln Landing
First Street/River Road
Rockport, IN

Lincoln Pioneer Village and Museum
Rockport, IN
(812) 649-9147
http://santaclausind.org/listings/lincoln-pioneer-village
-museum

Lincoln State Park
15476 County Rd 300 East
Lincoln City, IN
(812) 937-4710
https://in.gov/dnr/parklake/2979.htm

The Log Inn
12491 County Road 200 East
Haubstadt, IN
(812) 867-3216
http://theloginn.net

Ohio River Scenic Byway
www.ohioriverscenicroute.org
Spencer County Courthouse
200 Main Street
Rockport, IN
(812) 649-6027

Vincennes State Historic Sites
1 West Harrison Street
Vincennes, IN
(812) 882-7422
http://www.vincennescvb.org

Warrick County Courthouse
One County Square, Suite 200
Boonville, IN 47601
(812) 897-6160

LINCOLN IN ILLINOIS

A River Runs through It

The Lincolns came by land, leading oxen-pulled wagons loaded with all their belongings, a trip that took more than two weeks in wretched weather over horrendous roads. I instead make the drive north from Vincennes in under three hours on IL 121 to Decatur. It's another ten-minute drive to the Lincoln Trail Homestead State Park and Memorial where the family first settled in Illinois, but I decide to make the remainder of the journey by water, along the first leg of the eighty-five-mile Lincoln Heritage Water Trail on the Sangamon River flowing west from Decatur to Petersburg. Fall color is peaking, and jewel-bright leaves are reflected in the surface of the placid river as my friends and I launch our kayaks at Lincoln Park and paddle toward the 162-acre homestead.

Lincoln lived along the Sangamon and navigated its waters frequently in canoes and flatboats—it was at times the quickest and most convenient way to go. The trail's website claims that much of the scenery looks unchanged from two centuries ago, and though I wasn't around then, I'd have to agree. We paddle through large tracts of woods and watch leaves spin in circles as they dance down toward the water and drift slowly on the current.

Traveling together back then were Tom and Sarah, twenty-one-year-old Abe, and Sarah's two daughters and their husbands, including Dennis Hanks, who had married Sarah's oldest, also named Sarah. The family arrived at their new farmstead in March 1830 and built an eighteen-by-eighteen-foot log cabin, now long lost, but located roughly twelve miles southwest of Decatur in what is now the Lincoln Trail Homestead State Park and Memorial.

Whatever the Lincolns' hopes for a better life, it wasn't to be here. The corn crop went bad that summer, and malaria sickened several members of the family. Worse, the treacherous Winter of the Deep Snow followed, and animals and men died in the fiercest cold, ice, and snow in half a century.

Despite these calamities, Abe developed a romance.

Lincoln Read Law During Courting Visit

The Decatur Daily Review (Decatur, IL), Sunday, March 3, 1968

It may have started as courting visit paid by Young Abe Lincoln to Polly Warnick, the sheriff's daughter, one dull winter evening in 1830.

But what could have been a tragedy is now credited by some historians with starting the lanky pioneer on his interest in law that finally led him to the nation's highest office.

It was the winter of the big snow, when drifts covered the tops of rail fences, that Abe set out late in the afternoon for the Warnick place, several miles upriver and on the opposite bank.

In crossing the wintry stream, the 21-year-old got his feet wet but was apparently unaware of the danger until he was nearing his destination.

By the time he was safely in the Warnick's heart-warmed cabin, Lincoln's feet were frozen, and he was confined in bed there for more than a week.

During those long hours, Abe is said to have spent a good deal of his time reading the sheriffs law books—hardly a complete library and most of them from Indiana legislation.

While other travelers reportedly perished on the prairie that winter, Abe may have had a career born.

Oh, yes. Polly Warnick, evidently a popular lass, married Joseph Stevens.

Just a year later, by March 1831, Thomas and Sarah had decided to move on again, this time settling and buliding yet another cabin near Charleston in Coles County, about sixty-two miles southeast on IL 121. In an interesting twist of fate, twenty-seven years later on September 18, 1858, a crowd of twelve thousand, including eleven railroad cars of passengers from Indiana, would come to the Coles County Fairgrounds in Charleston to watch the fourth Lincoln debate against Stephen Douglas, a site that now includes the Lincoln Douglas Debate Museum.

NEW ORLEANS: FORETELLING THE FUTURE

Who would've known back then, when Lincoln left the farm and journeyed down the Sangamon River in a dugout canoe with his cousin John Hanks, that he was on his long road to greatness? The two headed to Sangamo Town, where they visited a tavern owned by Jacob Carman on Mill and Bridge Streets, one of the first businesses in the recently platted river town. They played cards and talked about an offer from Springfield storeowner Denton Offutt, who wanted them to pilot a flatboat to New Orleans loaded with his goods. The two liked the idea, accepted the offer, and met up with Lincoln's stepbrother, John Johnston, to begin work.

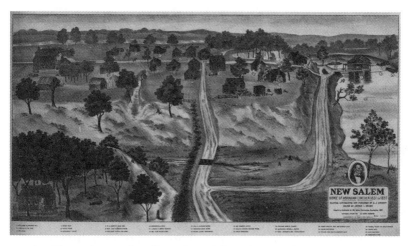

An old map showing the village of New Salem when Lincoln lived there between 1831 and 1837, with numbers marking where the Lincoln-Berry Store was located on Springfield Road and the site of the Rutledge Tavern and Store. *Photo courtesy of the Library of Congress*

The job entailed building the eight-by-eighteen-foot boat, for which Offutt paid them twelve dollars a month. For the sixteen-hundred-mile journey, they'd earn sixty dollars plus fifty cents a day. The launch didn't go smoothly, and a short distance downstream from Sangamo Town, northwest of Springfield, they ran aground at the milldam in New Salem. Lincoln made his way to shore and headed to a cooper shop owned by Henry Onstot to ask if he could borrow an augur, which they used to free the boat.

As on his last visit to New Orleans, Lincoln abhorred the scenes of slave auctions. His anger was so overwhelming that according to John Hanks, "We were afeared of getting into trouble about his talking so much, and we coaxed him with all our might to be quieter-like down there, for it wouldn't do any good nohow." Supposedly, and I'd love to believe this is true, the young men met up with a voodoo practitioner and fortune-teller who prophesized that Lincoln would become president "and all the Negroes will be free."

But before he could become president, Lincoln had to find a job. Returning to Illinois, he settled in New Salem, which at the time was booming, where he'd live for the next six years. He opened several stores, including one with Offutt and another—along with a tavern—with William Berry, thus becoming the only president to hold a liquor license. All eventually failed. Lincoln's other jobs in New Salem included running the post office and working as a surveyor. He also began studying law, and his interest in politics intensified.

The river was his passion. He'd spent his youth in Indiana and early adulthood in Illinois on the water, and one of his proposals was to clear and straighten the Sangamon River, making it navigable for commercial steamboats—a proposal that would have made New Salem an important port on the river. Also the only president to hold a US patent, Lincoln obtained one for a device designed to lift boats through shallow water, which would have helped New Salem and the Sangamon River become a viable route for steamships.

Alas, it wasn't to be. Ultimately, like Sangamo Town, New Salem started to fade when Petersburg, two miles away, became the county seat. By 1840 the settlement had been abandoned, its buildings falling into ruin and then, with time, disappearing altogether. Then in the early 1930s the Civilian Conservation Corps was put to work building Lincoln's New Salem, a replica of the village based on the original log homes, stores, mills, and school and a reconstructed Rutledge Tavern. Using costumed interpreters, exhibits, and authentic period furnishings, the village now showcases the time when Lincoln lived there. In one of those intriguing historic coincidences, Henry Onstot, who lent Lincoln his augur, had taken apart his cooper house in 1840 and moved it to Petersburg. More than a century later, it was dismantled and returned to Lincoln's New Salem, making it the only original building there.

Lincoln most likely never owned a home in New Salem; instead, he boarded with several families, including that of James Rutledge, the owner of a tavern and sawmill. It was there he met the auburn-haired and blue-eyed Ann Rutledge. Historians disagree on whether she was just an acquaintance, the love of his life, or somewhere in between. Here's what we know.

LOST LOVE

Born January 7, 1813, near Henderson, Kentucky, Ann Mays Rutledge was the third of ten children born to James Rutledge and his wife, Mary. In 1829, Rutledge and James Cameron built a dam, sawmill, and gristmill, laid out the village of New Salem, and began selling lots. It was common back then to build communities around mills and water sources, as mills were a gathering place for farmers who came to have their grain ground and homesteaders who needed wood sawn into planks. James Rutledge also opened a tavern, and that's where Lincoln lived when he came to New Salem—and where he met Ann. Described as beautiful, Ann was said to be about five feet, three inches tall and about 120 pounds. Her teeth were good (somewhat unusual back then), and she was sweet and well liked.

At the time she and Lincoln met, Ann was engaged to John McNamar, a handsome, well-to-do man worth between $10,000 and $12,000, who was considered the "catch of the village." McNamar traveled east to settle family business sometime between 1833 and 1834. On August 25, 1835, Ann died and was buried in the Old Concord Cemetery in rural Menard County. In 1890 her remains were moved to their current location in Petersburg, Illinois. Somewhere in the short time between McNamar's trip east and her death, she and Lincoln became romantically involved. In his book *Honor's Voice: The Transformation of Abraham Lincoln*, author Douglas L. Wilson writes that according to one of Ann's brothers, Lincoln "paid his addresses to Ann, continued his visits and attentions regularly and those resulted in an engagement to marry" (116). Another contemporary account from New Salem resident Benjamin F. Irwin said that Lincoln was "wofully in Love with a Remarkable handsome young Lady by the Name of Rutledge" (quoted in Wilson and Davis, *Herndon's Informants*, 325)

In the meantime, it seems McNamar may have been losing interest in Ann, no matter how lovely she was. Maybe once out east he became occupied with more cosmopolitan beauties, or maybe the mail service was bad; either way, his letters to her dwindled. What's a girl to do? In Ann's case, it seems, the most logical step was to break off the engagement. There were other men interested in her, so why wait around for someone so far away? It's an attitude I totally approve of.

One of Ann's enraptured followers described her thus: "This young lady was a woman of Exquisite beauty, but her intellect was quick-Sharp- deep & philosophic as well as brilliant. She had a gentle & kind a heart as an angl-full of love-kindness-sympathy. She was beloved by evry body and evry body respected and lovd her-so sweet & angelic was she. Her Character was more than good: it was positively noted throughout the County" (Wilson, *Honor's Voice*, 115).

Now to an interesting question. Gorgeous and sought after, why did Ann choose Lincoln over all the others? At the time, he wasn't yet an attorney. Consider what Ann's mother might have said about him as a potential husband. You know, the usual mom stuff: "He doesn't have a job, he's failed twice at running a store, his parents are as poor as dirt, he doesn't have any formal education, and he seems to move from place to place." He wasn't a handsome devil either. We don't know. Maybe Ann was able to recognize his potential and true worth, or maybe it wasn't much of a romance and was built up after Lincoln's death by Ann's family and others, including David Herndon, Lincoln's biographer and law partner who called Ann the love of Lincoln's life.

But was it one-sided? Wish we knew. No matter the degree of the relationship, it ended suddenly and sadly.

Summers were always a deadly time near the Sangamon in Illinois back then, and 1835 was particularly dreadful. A drenching rain in spring and summer caused latrines to overflow, contaminating the water supply. Then came humidity and high temperatures, breeding an overabundance of mosquitos. In all, it was a very bad combination. The mosquitos spread endemic malaria, and the bad water led to an outbreak of brain or bilious fever (what we now call typhoid). The deadly duo quickly killed a large number of people.

Lorenzo D. Matheny was quoted in Lewis Gannett's "The Ann Rutledge Story: Case Closed?" as saying:

> Spring and summer of 1835 was the hottest ever known in Illinois: from the first of March to the middle of July it rained almost every day, and the whole country was literally covered with water. When the rain ceased, the weather became excessively hot and continued so until sometime in August. About the 10th of August, the people began to get sick—lasted until October 1st—a number terminated fatally. Twelve practicing physicians in Springfield [population 1500] were continually engaged almost day and night. (53)

In mid-September, Matthew Marsh, who lived in New Salem, reported there weren't enough healthy people to care for the sick. Lincoln helped with the malaria victims until he too became sick.

As for Ann, some say she died within two days of contracting the disease and others that she lingered for a few weeks. Lincoln came to visit her as she lay dying, and people observing the two said they both cried knowing their romance was at an end.

Friend John Hill said Lincoln "was fearfuly [sic] wrought up on her death—My Father had to lock him up & keep guard over him for some two weeks I think, for fear he might Commit Suicide—The whole village engaged in trying to quiet him & reconcile him to the loss" (Gannett, "The Ann Rutledge Story," 47)

While he lived in New Salem, Lincoln often visited her grave, telling friends he hated to think of her lying in her grave alone. Whether he grieved for the rest of his life we cannot know, but rumors abounded about Lincoln's other romances. True or not, the stories certainly are salacious.

As for McNamar, he did return from his trip out east, and according to one account, in 1836, he evicted Ann's widowed mother from one of his properties after she couldn't pay the rent. Now on to the salacious rumors.

SAY IT AIN'T SO

Hannah Armstrong's husband Jack mercilessly teased Lincoln with the notion that Lincoln was having sex with Hannah. "It was a joke," informant James Taylor told Herndon in an interview conducted in 1865 or 1866. Jack Armstrong "plagued Abe terribly" with the ribald accusation that Lincoln had fathered one of Hannah's children. How did Jack Armstrong come up with such a joke? Lincoln spent time with Hannah at her home, enjoyed her company, and also enjoyed tending to her children. Perhaps this puzzled Jack. Why would a man savor that kind of companionship? In jest, apparently, Jack Armstrong jumped to a risqué conclusion. (Gannett, "The Ann Rutledge Story," 57)

It wasn't only Hannah Armstrong's babe who was said to have Lincoln as a father.

According to New Salem neighbor J. Rowan Herndon, Mrs. Abell, with whom Lincoln resided sometimes in New Salem, "has a daughter that is thought to Be Lincolns Child thay favor very much." (Gannett, "The Ann Rutledge Story," 57)

The rumor mill cranked on. In a village with a population of around 125, it was said that another wife of a New Salem resident "had a child—father uncertain—supposed to be Duncan's—or Lincoln's" (quoted in Wilson, *Honor's Voice*, 112–13)

Even if only one of these rumored children was fathered by Lincoln (and it could be none of them were), it raises an interesting question. Since the death of his great-grandson Robert Todd Lincoln Beckwith in 1985, except for rumors of an illegitimate child, no direct descendants of Lincoln are known to exist. But if he indeed fathered a child or two or three by these New Salem women, then there may indeed be direct descendants. And who knows? If he was that busy, maybe there were baby Lincolns in other towns. It does make one think, doesn't it?

THE FUTURE PRESIDENT'S WIFE

Lincoln was living in Springfield, having been elected to the Ninth Illinois Assembly, when twenty-year-old Mary Todd came to stay with her sister Elizabeth and her husband, Ninian W. Edwards, whose father was one of the first two US senators from Illinois and the third governor of Illinois. Mary's cousin John Stuart was Lincoln's law partner, and so the two moved in the same social circles. And, of course, people will talk.

Many thought it was poor match, and even Mary's sister Elizabeth Edwards said she "warned Mary that she and Mr. Lincoln were not suitable. Mr. Edwards and myself believed they were different in nature, and education and raising. They had no feelings alike. They were so different that they could not live happily as man and wife" (Baker, *Mary Todd Lincoln*, 89). But Mary was a belle, pretty and coquettish, and she captured several hearts—including that of Stephen Douglas, who also proposed marriage.

As a young beauty, freshly arrived in Springfield, Mary again famously declared her intention to marry a president. Her desire seems to fall in the category of "beware of what you wish for as it might come true." Her former dressmaker and confidante, Elizabeth Keckley (sometimes spelled Keckly), wrote of Mary's ambitions in her autobiography *Behind the Scenes: Or, Thirty Years a Slave and Four Years in the White House*, released in 1868.

But first a little bit about Keckley, who herself had a very interesting story to tell about her life. After decades of slavery, because of her social savvy, expert dressmaking skills, and sheer determination, she was able to purchase her freedom from her owners in St. Louis for $1200 in 1855 ($319,721.74 today). Making her way to Washington, DC, in 1860, she opened her own dressmaking business and soon had a list of influential clients including Varina Anne Banks Howell Davis, the wife of Jefferson Davis, the future president of the Confederacy, who at the time was the US senator from Mississippi. Davis liked Keckley's needlework so well she asked her to move south when the family left Washington. Move back to a slave state when the country was on the verge of civil war? Don't worry; Keckley was way smarter than that.

She seems to have developed a genuine fondness for Mrs. Davis, though, who was only eighteen when she married the thirty-six-year-old Davis in 1845. In her autobiography she wrote about her relationship with the Davis family.

> Since bidding them good-by at Washington, early in the year 1860, I have never met any of the Davis family. Years of excitement, years of bloodshed, and hundreds of thousands of graves intervene between the months I spent in the family and now. The years have brought many changes; and in view of these terrible changes even I, who was once a slave, who have been punished with the cruel lash, who have experienced the heart and soul tortures of a slave's life, can say to Mr. Jefferson Davis, "Peace! you have suffered! Go in peace." (73–74)

Also among the fashionable women Keckley met was Mary Lincoln, who loved fine clothing. The following year, after the inauguration, Keckley became Lincoln's modiste (fashionable dressmaker) as well as her companion. A purple velvet skirt with daytime bodice that Keckley designed for Mary Lincoln is on display at the National Museum of American History on Constitution Avenue in Washington, DC.

A Woman Who Knew What She Wanted

> Mrs. Lincoln from her girlhood up had an ambition to become the wife of a President. When a little girl, as I was told by one of her sisters, she was disposed to be a little noisy at times and was self-willed. One day she was romping about the room, making more noise than the nerves of her grandmother could stand. The old lady looked over her spectacles, and said, in a commanding tone:

"Sit down, Mary. Do be quiet. What on earth do you suppose will become of you if you go on this way?"

"Oh, I will be the wife of a President someday," carelessly answered the petted child. (Keckley, *Behind the Scenes*, 228–29)

A pretty and flirtatious belle when living in Springfield, Illinois, Keckley says Mary Todd was able to juggle numerous young suitors including two political rivals, Abraham Lincoln and Stephen A. Douglas, who were both vying for her hand in marriage. "The young lady was ambitious, and she smiled more sweetly upon Mr. Douglas and Mr. Lincoln than any of her other admirers, as they were regarded as rising men," writes Keckley. "She played her part so well that neither of the rivals for a long time could tell who would win the day. Mr. Douglas first proposed for her hand, and she discarded him" (Keckley, 229)

Keckley reports a "little chapter in a romantic history from the lips of Mrs. Lincoln herself" between the two of them where Douglas pleaded his cause:

> "Mary, you do not know what you are refusing. You have always had an ambition to become the wife of a President of the United States. Pardon the egotism, but I fear that in refusing my hand to-night you have thrown away your best chance to ever rule in the White House."
>
> "I do not understand you, Mr. Douglas," she is said to have responded.
>
> "Then I will speak more plainly. You know, Mary, that I am ambitious like yourself, and something seems to whisper in my ear, 'You will be President someday.' Depend upon it, I shall make a stubborn fight to win the proud position."
>
> "You have my best wishes, Mr. Douglas; still I cannot consent to be your wife. I shall become Mrs. President, or I am the victim of false prophets, but it will not be as Mrs. Douglas." . . .
>
> At one of the receptions at the White House, shortly after the first inauguration, Mrs. Lincoln joined in the promenade with Senator Douglas. He was holding a bouquet that had been presented to her, and as they moved along he said:

"Mary, it reminds me of old times to have you lean upon my arm."

"You refer to the days of our youth. I must do you the credit, Mr. Douglas, to say, that you were a gallant beau."

"Not only a beau, but a lover. Do you remember the night our flirtation was brought to an end?"

"Distinctly. You now see that I was right. I am Mrs. President, but not Mrs. Douglas."

"True, you have reached the goal before me, but I do not despair. Mrs. Douglas—a nobler woman does not live—if I am spared, may possibly succeed you as Mrs. President."

When Lincoln proposed just a few nights after Mary refused Douglas, Mary acted sassy with him as well. In another conversation via Todd to Keckley to us, she responded to his formally asking her to marry by telling him it was a bold move.

"Love makes me bold," he responded.

"You honor me, pardon me, but I cannot consent to be your wife."

"Is this your final answer, Miss Todd?" and the suitor rose nervously to his feet.

"I do not often jest, Mr. Lincoln. Why should I reconsider to-morrow my decision of to-day."

"Excuse me. Your answer is sufficient. I was led to hope that I might become dearer to you than a friend, but the hope, it seems, has proved an idle one. I have the honor to say good night, Miss Todd."

Pale in color but appearing to be calm, Lincoln bowed himself out of the room, losing his composure only after reaching his office. There he seemed frantic to his good friend, Dr. Henry, who came in to find him pacing the floor, obviously agitated.

When Henry asked what the matter was, Lincoln responded that he was sick of the world, found it to be a heartless, deceitful place and cared not how soon he was out of it.

"You rave," Henry supposedly responded. "What has happened? Have you been quarrelling with your sweetheart?"

And here again, we get Keckley's version of their conversation:

> "Quarrel! I wish to God it was a quarrel, for then I could look
> forward to reconciliation; the girl has refused to become my
> wife, after leading me to believe that she loved me. She is a
> heartless coquette."

> "Don't give up the conquest so easily. Cheer up, man, you may
> succeed yet. Perhaps she is only testing your love."

> "No! I believe that she is going to marry Douglas. If she does I
> will blow my brains out."

> "Nonsense! That would not mend matters. Your brains were
> given to you for different use. Come, we will go to your
> room now. Go to bed and sleep on the question, and you
> will get up feeling stronger to-morrow"; and Dr. Henry took
> the arm of his friend Lincoln, led him home, and saw him
> safely in bed. (229–34)

Lincoln wasn't able to sleep that evening and a doctor was called. It turns out Lincoln had a fever, and after he'd been confined to bed for a few days, the doctor became concerned enough that he called upon Mary Todd who was upset to find Lincoln was so ill. When she expressed a desire to go see him, the doctor said she'd been the one to cause his illness. To this Mary replied that she was only testing the sincerity of Lincoln's love for her, adding he was the idol of her heart and saying she would become his wife. Upon hearing the news, Lincoln improved quickly and within a few months he and Mary were married.

Keckley writes:

> I learned these facts from Dr. Henry and Mrs. Lincoln. I believe
> them to be facts, and as such have recorded them. They do not
> agree with Mr. Herndon's story, that Mr. Lincoln never loved
> but one woman, and that woman was Ann Rutledge; but then
> Mr. Herndon's story must be looked upon as a pleasant piece of
> fiction. When it appeared, Mrs. Lincoln felt shocked that one

who pretended to be the friend of her dead husband should deliberately seek to blacken his memory. Mr. Lincoln was far too honest a man to marry a woman that he did not love. He was a kind and an indulgent husband, and when he saw faults in his wife he excused them as he would excuse the impulsive acts of a child. In fact, Mrs. Lincoln was never more pleased than when the President called her his child-wife. (235–36)

Before the happy nuptials could take place, however, the couple broke up again, and Lincoln, though devastated, did manage to find some solace.

SARAH RICKARD

During a break in his romance with Mary Todd, Lincoln started attending parties and dances with a family friend named Sarah Rickard. He supposedly proposed to her, but he did so in such a way that she could not take the proposal seriously.

Sarah Rickard Barret: Letter to William H. Herndon: As exactly written, errors and all
Sarah Rickard Barret to William H. Herndon.
[August 12, 1888]
Sir
With a soar finger on my right hand I Get my Husband to do my writing. When I first met Mr Lincoln at Mr Butlers I was ten or twelve years of age. as I grew up he used to take me to little Entertainments the first was the Babes in the woods. he tooke me to the first Theater that ever played in Springfield. when I arrived at the age of 16 he became more attentive to me. I allway liked him as a friend but you know his pecular manner and his General deportment would not be likely to fasinate a young girl just entering the society world.
Mr Lincoln in after years used to say when I first met Sarah she was a little Girl wearing these Pantletts.
I agree with You that Mr Lincoln was very unfortunate in Marriage.

I remember very distinctly Thos[e] little Instances of our Young days.

Give my Respects to Your wife and accept the same to Your self
Sarah A Barret

Before he and Mary got back together, Lincoln was linked with two other women: Matilda Edwards of Springfield, Illinois, and Mary Curtis of Louisville, Kentucky. The latter was the recipient of a most unusual present, described here in Heritage Auction advertisement:

Lincoln purchased the blue enamel, diamond-studded, 18-karat gold timepiece offered in this lot. He had it engraved "To Miss Mary Todd from A.L. 1841" on the inside back cover. As the impending wedding grew nearer, Lincoln grew more moody and depressed, apprehensive of the coming event. According to accounts from W. H. Herndon, one of Lincoln's law partners, the guests and bride were present at the Edwards home on January 1, 1841, waiting; waiting for a bridegroom that would not show up. Others claim that this was only the day that Lincoln broke the engagement; no wedding was actually planned. Lincoln, in a March 1842 letter to his dear friend Joshua B. Speed, referred to this day, in part: "I am not going beyond the truth, when I tell you, that the short space it took me to read your last letter, gave me more pleasure, than the total sum of all I have enjoyed since that fatal first of Jany. '41. Since then, it seems to me, I should have been entirely happy, but for the never-absent idea, that there is one still unhappy whom I have contributed to make so. That still kills my soul. I can not but reproach myself, for even wishing to be happy while she is otherwise." Whichever is the true story, Lincoln never gave Miss Mary Todd the wedding present watch he had so thoughtfully picked out for her.

Returning to Springfield from a trip on January 14, 1841, Lincoln was at the home of William Butler where he boarded. A celebrated Kentucky beauty named Mary N. Curtis was visiting there at the time. They had met on several previous occasions and, on this particular day, they sat in the parlor and shared a pleasant conversation. With no warning, Lincoln pulled out the watch and presented it to Miss Curtis, saying something to the effect of "Mary, I've got something for you." He went on up the stairs to his room as she sat there stunned. Mary returned to her home in Louisville the next day, probably thinking she was engaged to an up-and-coming Illinois lawyer and politician. It was some time later, when she took the watch out to wind it, that Mary Curtis noticed the engraving, then realizing that Lincoln possibly just gave her the watch to rid himself of an unpleasant memory. The timepiece was placed away in a trunk for 31 years. In the meantime, Abraham Lincoln and Mary Todd did finally marry, on November 4, 1842.

What changed Lincoln's mind about marrying Mary Todd? One reason may be best summed up as follows: Ninian Edwards, who was married to Mary Todd's sister Elizabeth, said that she was "an alluring armful for a courageous man."

Who would have guessed?

CIRCUIT RIDER

In Springfield, Lincoln and his law partner, William Herndon, ran a two-man law firm, and Lincoln was considered the circuit partner. In that role, he visited the county seats throughout the Eighth Circuit when the circuit court was in session, a job entailing six months on the road—three months in the spring and three months in the fall. He traveled by horse and buggy or on horseback to the fifteen (later fourteen) counties on the circuit. Those county courthouses are part of Lincoln's Eighth Judicial Circuit, a trail that encompasses such places as the Greek Revival–style Mt. Pulaski Courthouse State Historic Site.

It took a full day's ride for Lincoln to travel the twenty-five miles from Springfield to the Mt. Pulaski courthouse, built in 1844 and just one of two of the circuit courthouses still remaining on their original sites. Lincoln visited the courthouse often, and the offices have been restored and are open for public tours. Unfortunately the court records of Lincoln's cases were destroyed by fire in 1857.

When the railroad bypassed Mt. Pulaski, the county seat moved to Lincoln, Illinois, and the circuit court along with it. As part of the Looking for Lincoln Heritage Coalition, a consortium of communities with sites that were important in Lincoln's life in Illinois have placed a series of illustrated markers telling the story of Lincoln's time practicing law in the area. These include the site of land he once owned, his former law office, and the Lincoln House Hotel in Lincoln, Illinois, named after the prominent attorney in 1854. The Lincoln House marker commemorates a meeting between artist Leonard Volk and Abraham Lincoln on the sidewalk in front of the hotel on July 16, 1858, during which Lincoln agreed to let Volk make his life mask. Another marker in Lincoln, the Lincoln Rustic Scene of Conspiracy, is named after a gang of counterfeiters who met at the Rustic Tavern at 412 Pulaski Street in 1876. Their plan was to steal Lincoln's body from his tomb in Springfield and hold it for ransom until they received payment of $200,000 and confirmed the release their engraver, who was serving time in the penitentiary. Thanks to good detective work, the plot was uncovered and Lincoln's body stayed where it was.

From Lincoln it's another sixty-four miles north on I-155 (more than a two-day journey in Lincoln's day) to reach the 1845 Metamora Courthouse State Historic Site in Metamora, Woodford County—the only other original Eighth Circuit courthouse still standing. In the eleven years Lincoln served as a circuit lawyer, he handled seventy circuit court cases there.

CLAYVILLE, ILLINOIS: THE BROADWELL INN

With the advent of the railroad in the late 1850s, travel became easier, but life on the road was still difficult. Sleeping options ranged from bedding in barns and fields to staying at inns of varying quality and comfort or finding a place in a farmer's home. It seems impossible now that Lincoln—or any lawyer—could go into a courtroom and win a case after spending the night sleeping on the back of his horse under a tree to get out of the rain. But he did. As hard as all that traveling must have been, it helped Lincoln tremendously by boosting name recognition and popularity and also earned him a wide range of clients, such as John Broadwell and his family.

"We don't know that Abraham Lincoln stayed here but he rode the circuit and so would have passed through here often," says Dan Usherwood, president of Pleasant Plains Historical Society, which manages the Clayville Historic Site just twelve miles from Lincoln's New Salem. "But there's no registry so we can't prove it."

It does seem very likely that Lincoln would have taken a meal and stayed at the Broadwell Inn, the second-oldest brick building in the state. Built in 1825 by the Broadwell family, who arrived in this area of Illinois via the Illinois River in 1819, the inn served as a stagecoach stop and tavern. Back then, travelers were divided by sex into two separate parlors.

"In the men's parlor there would have been a whiskey barrel, boot pullers to help the men get their boots off, and spittoons," says Usherwood, emphasizing that their buildings are original and not replicas. "Men would have smoked, chewed tobacco, sipped whiskey, and cussed. On the other side of the wall, the room would have been more elaborately decorated with padded chairs, and there probably would have been a cradle for women traveling with babies." But no whiskey barrel or spittoons, darn it.

"Any light would have come from the windows, whale oil lanterns, or the fireplace," continues Usherwood. "Kerosene lanterns didn't come along until the 1870s." Upstairs mattresses would have rested on ropes, which would be turned to tighten them—hence the saying "sleep tight." "You didn't rent a bedroom, you didn't rent a bed," says Usherwood about life on the road for travelers back then. "You rented a space. People often slept four to a bed and slept horizontally so you could squeeze more people in." If that sounds rough, Usherwood points out that many travelers slept along the road with no shelter at all and little to separate their bodies from the ground. It was not a pampered way to travel. And this would have been the life of Abraham Lincoln, who as a lawyer, politician, and candidate was away from home for half the year.

Cooking at the Broadwell Inn was done over a large wood-burning fireplace. A tripod would be placed over the fire, and a chicken, strung up by a rope, would roast over the fire. Clayville cooks also used a trammel, an adjustable pothook used to hang cooking pots over the fire at different heights, which could be swung in and out to adjust the heat. Another cooking instrument was the inn's large beehive oven. Coals from the fireplace were placed on the floor of the oven, and after it heated up, it could be used for baking cakes, breads, and pies.

So, what would have been served at the Broadwell Inn? Cabbages, corn, and whatever else was growing in the garden. Pork. Beef might grace the table every once in a while, when cattle herded from farms further north passed by on their way to St. Louis. Travelers like Lincoln would have been served soups, stews, and ham with beans, all staple tavern fare. There wasn't necessarily a menu—you ate what was available whether you liked it or not.

The meals Lincoln ate in taverns, which could range from good to poor, and his meager fare at home were a sharp contrast to the foods the family of his future wife ate. In the best traditions of upper-crust Kentucky cuisine, home-cured hams, gravies, fried chicken, spoonbread, johnnycakes, fried okra, butter beans, squab, woodcock, turkey, potpies, custards, cakes, and rich puddings would have been staples at the Todds, not once in a while treats.

We can't confirm that Lincoln stayed at the Broadwell, but we know he worked as an attorney for the Broadwell family, and Jerry Smith, a direct descendent of the Broadwells, says the family kept him busy. "He represented John Broadwell on at least four cases," says Smith, who is pretty sure Lincoln visited the Broadwell Inn both as an attorney and as he traveled the road to Virginia and Beardstown, among other towns on the circuit. "Where else would he have eaten and stayed?"

According to Smith, Moses Broadwell founded Sangamo Town, creating eighty lots with the idea it would become the county seat of Sangamon County. Its name was changed to Clayville in honor of Henry Clay. Smith also states, "Lincoln stayed with Charles Broadwell at Sangamo Town when he was building the raft that he used to go to New Salem and then to New Orleans."

THE DEBATES

It's a late fall day when I drive the Bement-Monticello Road (now IL 105), a straight and narrow ribbon of asphalt bisecting flat planes of farmland, toward Bement, a small village just thirty-four miles from Decatur. Normally, Bement, population 1,696, wouldn't be on my list of places to go. But events transpired here that would be momentous not only for the famous men involved, but also, several years later, for the nation.

In 1858, candidate Abraham Lincoln wrote to incumbent Illinois Senator Stephen Douglas, his rival in love and politics, challenging him to a series of debates. Family lore says Bement businessman and politician Francis Everett Bryant, a friend of Douglas and an admirer of Lincoln, invited the two to plan the debates at his home, now the Bryant Cottage State Historic Site. Douglas was likely at Bement's when he wrote to accept Lincoln's challenge, and the fame Lincoln won during the debates helped him secure the Republican presidential nomination and run against and beat Douglas in the presidential race of 1860.

The men agreed to hold the Lincoln-Douglas debates (or the Great Debates of 1858) in seven different locations throughout the state. The first took place just three weeks later on August 21 in Ottawa, a city on the Illinois River 125 miles north of Bement. It was held at Washington Square, and the site now features bronze statues of the debaters as well as a reflecting pool. There are similarities among many of the sites—statuary, interpretative markers, and wayside signs—but each is unique as well, offering a sense of the turnings of history brought about by the debates and the knowledge that if Douglas hadn't foolishly agreed to them, Lincoln might never have become president.

Trying to follow the debate trail in chronological order is like playing pinball—ricocheting north and south, east and west, and then back again. I wonder how Lincoln and Douglas did it in the days of riverboat, rail, and horseback travel. Traveling another 108 miles northwest of Ottawa takes me to Freeport (about two hours west of Chicago), where on August 27 the second debate attracted over fifteen thousand people—not bad for a town with a population of five thousand at the time. The self-interpretative site at Freeport leads past a series of wayside signs recounting the events and ideas that led up to the debates as well as life-size statues of the two debaters.

It's a much longer trek to where the third debate was held, over six hours south to Union County Fairgrounds and the Lincoln Memorial Park in Jonesboro. So instead of traveling there directly, I study my map and decide to head to Vandalia first, the Illinois state capital for three years before it was moved to Springfield. The journey is still long, about four and a half hours south on IL 39, but there's a lot to see in southern Illinois. Lincoln received his law degree in Vandalia and practiced law in the imposing white brick Federal-style building that is now the Vandalia State House Historic Site. Built in 1836 and on the National Register of Historic Places, the state house was a last-ditch effort to keep Vandalia as the state capital. But in this case, when they built it, they didn't come. The following year, Springfield made the cut. The Vandalia State House still has the distinction of being the oldest state capitol building still standing in the state, even though Illinois has had three capitals—the first, in Kaskaskia was washed away by the Mississippi River.

Traveling through southern Illinois is surprisingly pretty. The flat farmland of the north and central part of the state gradually swells into undulating tree-covered hills, stony bluffs, large tracts of woods, and beautiful vistas. It's less than two hours south to Equality in Gallatin County and well worth the trip, if just for the view. But there's more here: Equality has a macabre history.

SIDE TRIP TO EQUALITY: SALT MINES, SLAVERY, AND THE REVERSE UNDERGROUND RAILROAD

Located on the north side of the Saline River, a tributary of the Ohio River, the town of Equality was at one time the county seat of Gallatin and home of John Crenshaw. Crenshaw owned the leases for mining salt at the Great Salt Springs, located just a short way from Equality. Through rigorous research on period documents, historians such as Jon Musgrave have discovered that Crenshaw not only owned slaves, he also ran a reverse Underground Railroad.

He was able to do the former because though Illinois was a free state, in the early 1800s a special law let salt miners like Crenshaw own slaves because, so they argued, they couldn't find laborers willing to do the work for pay—probably because they didn't want to pay them enough for such punishing work. This was the flip side of why laborers like Thomas Lincoln abhorred slavery and left Kentucky, a slave state: they felt they couldn't compete with what was basically free labor. In 1820, the Gallatin County census listed 239 slaves or servants. The population in general for that year in Gallatin County was 3,155.

Salt mining was backbreaking work. Hence the saying "back to the salt mines."

At its peak, the business of making salt required hundreds of workers. Since vast amounts of firewood were required to boil the saltwater, the workforce included tree cutters and crews to split and transport firewood to the constantly burning fires at the salt spring. Envisioning this demand for wood fuel, the thousands of acres of "salt reservations" the government had set aside included thousands of acres of timber required for the boiling operation. As indicated by the massive investment of energy and labor required for salt production, salt in America was not the inexpensive commodity we know and take for granted today. Our essential need for salt, whatever its cost, is why the production of salt at this Illinois source continued even after all of the trees within a mile of the site had been cut down for firewood. (Illinois Department of Natural Resources, "When Salt Was Gold," 12)

Once the local sources of firewood were exhausted, a wooden pipeline was built to carry the saltwater several miles away to new location where there were trees to fuel the fires to boil the brine into salt for shipment.

Crenshaw, who built a large mansion about five miles from Equality called Hickory Hills, had other business dealings besides salt mining. In his reverse Underground Railroad operation, he and his cohorts kidnapped free blacks and sold them into slavery, transporting them downriver to the Deep South, where opportunities for escape and legal recourse were few. Crenshaw kept his captives on the third floor of his house, where they were chained, beaten, raped, and tortured before being sold. He is also accused of breeding his captives to increase his stock of potential slaves for selling—an unbelievably evil type of entrepreneurship that made him very wealthy. In the downstairs of his opulent home, Crenshaw and his family lived lavishly, and, as he was politically connected, they had all the right sorts of people visit, including Abraham Lincoln when he was a rising star politician and attorney.

No one believes that Lincoln or many of the people who visited Crenshaw in what is now called the Slave House knew what was going on, says Musgrave, who has written extensively on the subject in news and journal articles as well as in his books, *The Real Story of the Old Slave House and America's Reverse Underground* and *Slaves, Salt, Sex & Mr. Crenshaw*.

"Crenshaw designed the upstairs to hold slaves who were in transit," says Musgrave. "If Crenshaw acted like the other slave traders, he needed a holding place because he kidnapped several people at a time and held them until he had enough to ship them down south."

According to Musgrave, Lincoln was speaking on the campaign trail in Gallatin in 1840 as a surrogate for William Henry Harrison. "He did a campaign through southern and Central Illinois," says Musgrave. "Everywhere he went, he held a rally or debate. He went to Shawneetown, which was the trade center of the area. He was admitted to the bar in Vandalia at the courthouse. He was down there for twelve days except for one night when he went to Morgantown, Kentucky. He spoke in Equality and stopped to get his breath. During that time he visited the Old Slave House. There are references to Crenshaw holding a big party there. There were doors that could be folded open to make space for 80 or so people."

The perfect party house. What a host.

The Crenshaw Home, reputed to be seriously haunted, is now a historic site and is undergoing renovations. Musgrave has been in the home and describes its ambience as very unsettling. "It's spooky," he says, noting that there have been several exorcisms, the second one conducted by the same exorcists who did the house in Amityville.

As for hauntings, what else would you expect given all the horror, anguish, and pain experienced in the home? If there's any justice, it's provided in an old photo of Crenshaw with a crutch and the accompanying story. Crenshaw needed the crutch because one of his prisoners attacked him with an axe, severely injuring his leg, in retaliation for the rape of several kidnapped women.

South of Shawneetown there was another station on the reverse Underground Railroad. Here victims were imprisoned in cells in the basement, most likely shackled to the large iron rings set into walls discovered there. Slaves were also said to be kept in a cave near the home of one of Shawneetown's prominent residents, a man identified as "Mr. John C."

According to Musgrave, Crenshaw owned another building in Equality, the Lane Tavern, which still stands and is now a private residence.

Now empty and seemingly isolated in what was once the booming river port of Shawneetown, the three-story Greek Revival–style Shawneetown Bank was constructed in 1839–1841 and is on the National Register of Historic Places. Not open for tours, it's a beautiful building with a limestone front facade, portico, and steps. It's well worth a drive-by look.

BACK TO THE DEBATES . . . AND LINCOLN PARK

From Equality, I pass by national and state forests and numerous lakes on my way to Jonesboro, south of the Mason-Dixon Line, where, on September 15, Lincoln and Douglas held their third debate in front of fifteen hundred people. Musgrave told me the site is now part of the Shawnee National Forest's Lincoln Park. The sylvan setting includes the Lincoln Memorial pond and several walking trails and is described as a great habitat for turtles, although I don't see any that day. The Shawnee National Forest is gorgeous: all big boulders, cliffs, lakes, deep dark forests, and plunging waterfalls. Although I miss the turtles, I do see deer, including bucks with huge antlers, which quite makes up for it.

The next twelve miles on IL 146 meander through another enormous swath of woods that includes, according to my map, the Trail of Tears State Forest, the Union County State Fish & Wildlife Area, and the Brown Barrens Nature Preserve. I'm getting really close to the Mississippi River here as it courses north, dividing Illinois from Missouri—a (mostly) free state from a slave state. It's the Mississippi that slaves needed to cross to get to freedom, which affected a lot of the towns and cities along its banks.

The Postville Courthouse State Historic Site, built in what is described as an austere French style (think seriously plain), served as the Logan County government from 1840 to 1848. In one of life's ironies, the original courthouse can now be seen in Greenfield Village in Dearborn, Michigan. The people in Logan County had to build a replica.

I enjoy old buildings, but another important part of all this driving, following both the debates and the Eighth Circuit Court, is that it gives you the scope of Lincoln's travels and the uniqueness—which must have been magnified tenfold before chains and interstates—of each region he visited. Near Postville, a new town was platted called Lincoln (yes, named after him before he became president—the only town to do so), and in 1853 Lincoln was asked to christen the selling of lots for the new town. That christening, according to a Looking for Lincoln Story Trail Wayside titled "Lincoln's Lincoln," was somewhat unique. Lifting the covering off a pile of watermelons stacked on the ground, Lincoln picked one up, sliced it open, and then squeezed some of its juice into a tin cup. After giving a speech, he used the juice to christen the town—an event now marked by a monument of a giant watermelon.

On November 21, 1860, president-elect Lincoln gave a speech in Lincoln on his way to Chicago. Less than five years later, on May 3, 1865, his funeral train stopped there as it made its way to Springfield where he was buried.

FRENCH CONNECTIONS

It's fifty-four miles driving north on IL 3 through what's called the French Colonial Country of the Middle Mississippi River Valley—a collection of hamlets dotting the banks of the Mississippi River. French was the language of choice for the first European settlers who came here in the 1600s. Examples of French architectural styles abound, and while I marvel at what I see on the trip, it's Ellis Grove that's on my itinerary. I'm heading to where Lincoln dined with his friend Pierre Menard, whose beautiful French Colonial–style home is now the Pierre

Abraham Lincoln visited the home of Pierre Menard, considered one of the finest examples of French Colonial architecture in Illinois and now a state historic site. *Photo courtesy of Wiki Commons*

Menard Home State Historic Site. Overlooking the Mississippi River, the two-story house with its multiple porches is centered on extensive gardens, including a small historic herb and vegetable garden located near the kitchen. The ground level is a museum, and the first and second floors are living spaces decorated with furnishings reflective of a wealthy businessman's taste—Menard was a fur trader, businessman, and presiding officer of the Illinois Territorial Legislature, serving from 1818 to 1822 as the first lieutenant governor.

On the National Register of Historic Places and designated a national historic landmark, the home has a gracious feel, and views of the grounds and river from the wraparound porch and windows make one long to just sit and sip—maybe a mint julep, as we are somewhat south—and while away the day. Outbuildings include a stone kitchen with a "restored" brick baking oven that's connected to the house by a covered walkway, a reconstructed brick smokehouse, a replica of a stone springhouse, and the enchantingly named but less-than-romantic poteau sur solle (post-on-sill construction) structure that was the family privy.

Regretfully leaving Pierre's home behind, I steer north on IL 3 again to the intriguingly named Cahokia Courthouse. The name, I learn, is from the Illinois Indian word meaning "wild birds." The courthouse, now in the periphery of St. Louis but at one time more wild and remote, was built as a private residence in 1740 using a construction style known as French Creole poteaux-sur-solle (post-on-sill), which was used by French settlers who immigrated from Normandy in northern France. The style is quite rare; only about thirty edifices built in that style exist today in the United States. If you're really into log cabin construction, which I'm actually getting to be, here's a description from the Great River Road webpage for the courthouse: "In this method upright hewn logs are seated on a horizontal log sill and the spaces between the logs are filled with stone and mortar chinking. This type of construction is different from the more familiar horizontal Anglo-American style." Now you know, and if you happen to come across one of the thirty remaining buildings, you can impress your friends with your knowledge. Interestingly, the Cahokia Courthouse, one of the oldest state historic sites, dating back to Illinois' French colonial heritage, has gotten around. It was taken apart, moved, and rebuilt several times over the years before the state returned it to its original foundation.

Besides Lincoln, some other familiar names pop up along the southern Illinois-Missouri border. The French had surrendered the area to the British, and we wanted it back. So on July 4, 1778, George Rogers Clark and his "Long Knives" captured the town of Kaskaskia and Fort Gage. It wasn't much of a battle as no shots were fired. Clark, as you may recall, won the Battle of Vincennes too. It was all part of the strategy to make the Northwest Territory part of the American Republic. Fort Gage came into play again when it provided men, supplies, and

The Great River Road follows the Mississippi River, passing through some of the earliest settlements in Illinois. The Old Cahokia Courthouse, now a historic site in St. Clair County, is the oldest remaining courthouse in the state. Lincoln practiced law and campaigned for William Henry Harrison here. *Photo courtesy of Enjoy Illinois*

information to Clark's younger brother William and his friend Meriwether Lewis when they passed through in 1803. The two were leading the Corps of Discovery Expedition on the way to the Northwest.

Several taverns once stood along the Vincennes–St. Louis Trail, perfect places for Clark and his men to stop. Just outside of Iuka the Halfway Tavern, dating back to 1815 and reconstructed in the 1970s, is so named because it stands near the midpoint of the trail. Lincoln may have stayed here, as it was a stagecoach stop. According to historic accounts, an enterprising group of Indians robbed gold from a passing stagecoach sometime in the early 1800s and buried it in a wooded area north of the tavern. If that's true, so far no one has found it (or at least no one has admitted to finding it). It's approximately eighty-four miles straight east on US 50 from Cahokia to Iuka and somewhat out of the way, as the next part of our journey takes us north along the Mississippi, first to Alton and then to

Alton, Illinois, a river city on the Mississippi, was the scene of the last debate between Lincoln and Stephen Douglas. *Photo courtesy of Enjoy Illinois*

Quincy, both river ports, important stops on the Underground Railroad, and hotbeds of abolitionists. The drive from Cahokia to Alton is just thirty-eight minutes north on I-255, and I pull into this charming river town just as the sun is setting over the Mississippi River.

ALTON: THE FINAL DEBATE AND A DUEL

On their way to Washington, DC, in October 1847, then US Representative Lincoln and his family traveled through Alton. Lincoln also visited on March 27, 1849, on his way back from serving in Congress. August 5 found him in the city again as he journeyed to Terre Haute, Indiana, and that same year, on October 2, Lincoln gave a speech in front of the Presbyterian Church there. But Lincoln is most remembered in Alton for his final debate with Stephen Douglas on October 15, recreated in bronze in downtown Alton.

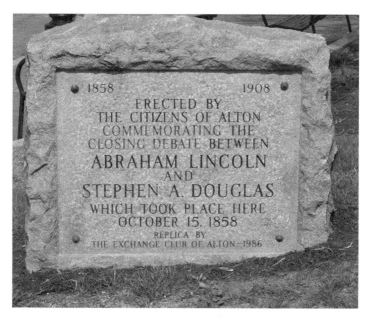

A marker shows where the debate took place. Alton was also a stop on the Underground Railroad. *Photo courtesy of Enjoy Illinois*

The two orators arrived in Alton at five o'clock on the morning of their debate aboard the *City of Louisiana*. Leaving the dock, Douglas went to the Alton House hotel and Lincoln to the Franklin House hotel, one of the city's finest, which was located at 206 State Street. The building is still standing and now is known as the Lincoln Lofts. Also arriving at the Franklin House was Mary Lincoln, who had traveled by train from Springfield. Aboard the same train were members of the Springfield Cadets, a group that included the Lincolns' oldest son, Robert, and Senator Lyman Trumbull. Lincoln also used the Franklin House Hotel as his campaign headquarters.

Though he didn't speak of it, Alton was where James Shields, the state auditor of Illinois, challenged Lincoln to a duel because of a series of letters published in the *Sangamon Journal* calling Shields a "conceit dunce" as well as a fool and a liar. Signed "Rebecca," the letters had been written by Lincoln, his wife, Mary, and Julia Jayne, who would become the wife of Senator

Trumbull. As the one challenged, Lincoln got to choose his weapon and selected a cavalry broadsword "of the largest size."

"I didn't want the d——d fellow to kill me, which I think he would have done if we had selected pistols," Lincoln later explained.

The two arranged to meet on Sunshine Island, closer to the Missouri side of the Mississippi River, as dueling hadn't been outlawed there yet. Lincoln, standing six feet four compared to Shields five feet three, is said to have demonstrated his overwhelming advantage by reaching up and slicing off the branch of a willow tree blocking their way. It was enough for Shields, who agreed to drop his challenge in return for a written apology for writing the letters.

As the boat made its way to the mainland, Lincoln, a practical joker, lay down in the bottom of the boat, pulling a sheet of oilcloth over him. Many of those waiting on shore broke into tears, believing he was dead. They were not pleased when he jumped up to surprise them. Neither was the local newspaper, and they chastised him in the next day's edition.

As for Shields, who made the wise decision not to fight Abe, he went on to become a brigadier in the Army of the Potomac, and in March 1862 helped defeat Stonewall Jackson in the Battle of Kernstown in the Shenandoah Valley campaign. It was Jackson's only defeat. The president, his old adversary, promoted Shields to major general.

Sunshine Island's pretty name was later changed to the much less appealing Smallpox Island when it became the site of a hospital where Confederate soldiers incarcerated at Alton's military prison were sent when they developed the disease. Few soldiers who were quarantined on the island survived. A monument marks the graves of 260 Confederate prisoners buried there.

Following the Lincoln & Civil War Legacy Trail in Alton takes me to My Just Desserts, a lovely restaurant in the old Ryder Building at 31 East Broadway. In Lincoln's time, the Ryder Building served as a courthouse and may have been the site of the politically charged Lovejoy murder trial.

Lincoln had been an ardent supporter of Elijah Parish Lovejoy, the courageous publisher of an abolitionist newspaper who in 1837 was murdered by an angry proslavery mob who threw his printing press into the river. Lovejoy, buried in the Alton City Cemetery at Fifth Street and Monument Avenue, is said to haunt his burial ground.

In 1840, Lincoln delivered a speech at the Ryder Building in support of Whig candidate William Henry Harrison. Later, as attorney for Simeon Ryder, owner of the building, Lincoln helped collect an old debt. The 1844 original letter Lincoln wrote and signed telling Ryder he'd won his case is preserved at the Hayner Public Library with its multivolume collection of Abraham Lincoln references.

Lincoln also tried the 1857 case, *Macready v. City of Alton*. Mary Macready, an Irish immigrant and Shakespearean actress who lived in New York, was walking down an Alton street undergoing construction when she fell into a hole and badly injured her ankle, leg, and back, and Lincoln demanded $20,000 for her damages. Unfortunately, the jury awarded her only $300.

US Senator Lyman Trumbull, who, like Lincoln, abhorred slavery, lived in a one-and-a-half-story red brick gable-roofed residence with a full basement and limestone foundation at 1105 Henry Street in Alton. It's still a private home and a national historic landmark. There's no record Lincoln was ever here, but given they were such good friends, it's hard to believe he wasn't. An interpretative marker is located near the house in Haskell Park, at the corner of Henry and Twelfth Streets.

QUINCY: THE SIXTH DEBATE AND HISTORIC HOMES

Leaving Alton a day later, I wind north along I-72, catching glimpses of the bluffs along the Mississippi River. It's a little over two hours to the Lincoln-Douglas Debate Plaza in Quincy's Washington Park, where the next-to-last debate was held on

October 13. It wasn't the first time Lincoln had visited this quaint river town. Four years earlier, he gave a speech there denouncing slavery.

"Washington Park, the sixth debate site of 1858, is still Quincy's hub for downtown," says Lori Tuttle, public relations and marketing manager at the Quincy Area Convention & Visitors Bureau. "So there's the historic tie-in, but a nice interlocking of current events happen there such as free Blues in the District, concerts all summer, the Farmer's Market, and Lincoln in the District Festival each June. That's a rather new event, only a couple years old, and gaining in popularity each year."

Well-known sculptor Lorado Taft, known for his beautiful fountains in Chicago, designed the bas-relief sculpture commemorating the debate. It's a stop on the city's Lincoln Heritage Trail that also includes the Lincoln-Douglas Debate Interpretative Center—an exploration of the growth of slavery in the United States and the ways both Douglas and Lincoln attempted to combat it.

Walking one block south of the square, I wait for the tour of the recently restored 1835 Dr. Richard Eells House to begin. The two-story red brick home, four blocks from the Mississippi River, was the first stop on the Underground Railroad for runaway slaves. In a related aside, Eells was transporting an escaped slave named Charley who had been rescued while swimming across the Mississippi when the two encountered a posse looking for the escapee. Eells told Charley to run, which he did, but unfortunately he was captured and returned to Missouri. Eells was arrested and appeared in front of Judge Stephen Douglas (yes, that Douglas), who fined him $400 (over $12,000 today). Eells, who is credited with helping hundreds of slaves escape, appealed the case. Decided against him in 1850, his appeal was the only documented Underground Railroad case to come before the US Supreme Court.

The stately white John Wood Mansion at Twelfth and State Streets in Quincy is one of the first Greek Revival–style homes built in the Midwest. John Wood made his fortune as a land

The John Wood Mansion was built between 1835 and 1838. As twelfth governor of Illinois, Wood supported fellow Republican Abraham Lincoln in his 1860 presidential campaign. *Photo courtesy of the Quincy Area Convention & Visitor's Bureau*

speculator, buying and selling off plots in downtown Quincy as the town grew. In the mid-1830s Wood saw another opportunity when skilled German immigrant craftsmen started to migrate north to the St. Louis area. Wood, who was fluent in German, recruited them to build his mansion, trading more land for their labor and settling much of the south side of Quincy with

Germans immigrants. Wood rose in the ranks of local politics from alderman to governor before joining the Civil War effort as quartermaster general of Illinois and colonel of the 137th Illinois Regiment. It's not likely that Lincoln ever stayed at the Wood mansion, but, as governor, Wood let fellow Republican Lincoln use his office in Springfield during the 1860 presidential campaign. The restored John Wood Mansion is open to the public.

Before leaving Quincy, I walk through the 1800s Lincoln-era Log Cabin Village on Quinsippi Island Park, studying five original log structures transported to the site, including three cabins, a church, and a corn crib, as well as a stone smokehouse. All again remind me of how glad I am not to be a pioneer.

The debates did not win Lincoln the senate seat. Douglas held on. But Lincoln, who took the position that the United States could not survive as half slave and half free, defeated Douglas for the presidency two years later.

GALENA

Another Captain Lincoln

Driving north from Quincy, I take a step back into a different facet of early Illinois history—a war for land and a way of life.

In 1832, about one thousand Native American warriors and civilians crossed the Mississippi into northern Illinois in an attempt to regain land lost during a treaty signed in 1804. Leading the group was Black Hawk, a Sauk leader who previously fought against immigrant Americans during the War of 1812. As typical when it came to treaties, the Indians got the short end of the deal. In exchange for $2,234.50 plus a $1,000 annuity and the right to live on their land until it was sold, the Sauk and Fox turned over fifty million acres to the United States. But upon returning from their winter hunt in 1829, the Indians found that masses of prospectors attracted by a lead rush in the Galena area had taken over their land, forcing them to leave Illinois and move across the Mississippi. Needless to say, they were angry.

War broke out, and Black Hawk and his soldiers went on the attack. Near the Apple River, just a few miles from the Mississippi River port city of Galena, a fort was hastily assembled in just under a week. Back in New Salem, Lincoln volunteered to serve in the Illinois Militia. Elected captain of his first company, Lincoln was present in the aftermath of two of the war's battles, where he helped bury the militia dead, including those killed when Black Hawk attacked the fort at Apple River. After the war, no longer needed, the fort was allowed to fall into ruins. Now the Apple River Fort State Historic Site, replicated using findings from an archaeological dig, it's worth a detour for those visiting Galena, just about ten minutes away.

The City on the Hill

It's easy to see why visitors flock to Galena—the whole town is picture-perfect with charming Victorian-era buildings lining the streets and creating a transcendent charm. In the early evening in particular, it's easy to imagine Lincoln riding in a hansom cab or walking to visit friends in some of the many period manses in Galena now open to the public.

I could walk or drive, but instead I hop aboard the Galena Trolley Tour for a two-and-a-half-hour exploration of three of the most historic of these houses—the home of President Ulysses S. Grant, Lincoln's general during the Civil War; the Belvedere Mansion and Gardens; and the Dowling House. The three homes differ widely in style. First there's the solidly limestone Dowling House, the oldest home in Galena, which is really saying something for a place with an abundance of historic buildings; its first floor was once a trading post with the family living above. The Grant home, a red brick structure with a cleverly angled front entrance and about 90 percent of the original furnishings, is adorable. But the crown jewel of the tour and Galena is the extraordinarily opulent twenty-two-room, five-thousand-square-foot Italianate Belvedere Mansion and

The home of President Ulysses Grant in Galena, Illinois. General Grant served under Lincoln during the Civil War, and the two also knew each other in Galena, a beautiful river port city. *Photo courtesy of Wikimedia*

Gardens, built in 1857 as the home of J. Russell Jones, a steamboat captain and US ambassador to Belgium.

Jones was a big supporter of Grant in his rise to the presidency. Lincoln often called on Jones after he became president, interested in learning if Grant was going to run against him in the next election. As president, Lincoln appointed Jones as US marshal for the Northern District of Illinois, and after Lincoln's assassination, Jones served as a pallbearer for his funeral train procession in Chicago.

Not included in the tour but worth a stop is the 1843 Greek Revival–style home belonging to Elihu B. Washburne, an attorney and US Congressman who was political adviser to both Lincoln and Grant and later US ambassador to France. Located

Built in 1857 by J. Russell Jones, a steamboat captain whom Lincoln appointed as ambassador to Belgium, the spectacular Belvedere Mansion stands out even among the many historic homes in Galena. *Photo courtesy of Wikimedia*

next door to the Belvedere Mansion, it too played an important part in Lincoln's connection to Galena.

Also enjoy lunch or even spend the night at the historic DeSoto House, billed as the "Largest Hotel in the West" when it opened on April 9, 1855. The DeSoto became a hub for the many visitors swarming to this important river port and was quite the thing with its 225 guest rooms, a gentleman's reading room, ladies' parlors, a three-hundred-seat dining hall, and a kitchen capable of feeding hundreds. It had its own gasworks for lighting halls, dining rooms, and public areas, and it also offered retail stores, offices, a saloon, and a bowling alley.

Ulysses S. Grant used rooms 209 and 211 in the DeSoto House for his campaign headquarters during his presidential campaigns, and he was not the only politician to take advantage of the luxurious hotel with its velvet carpets, rosewood furniture,

Lincoln campaigned for president at the DeSoto House Hotel in Galena in 1860. The historic hotel was built in 1855 and is still in business in beautiful downtown Galena. *Photo courtesy of Enjoy Illinois*

marble-topped tables, satin damask curtains, and double-round seven-octave carved rosewood pianoforte. In support of John Fremont's bid for the presidency, Lincoln spoke from the hotel's Main Street balcony on July 23, 1856. Two years later, Stephen A. Douglas would stand on the same balcony to give a speech. Then, in another two years, on September 13, 1860, a crowd of over fifteen thousand rallied in front of the Desoto to support Lincoln's presidential bid.

CHICAGOLAND

I'm traveling through Oak Brook, a prosperous Chicago suburb some thirty minutes from downtown (depending, of course, on how awful the traffic is, and let's face it; Chicago traffic is always awful, except maybe at midnight) when, turning a corner, I'm suddenly back in the 1850s. I brake, almost causing a pileup of fast-moving cars behind me, and make a quick left turn across

Frederick Graue's Mill in Oak Brook was a well-documented stop on the Underground Railroad. At one time, mills could be found on many rivers and streams and were used for sawing wood and grinding grain into flour and meal. They were also social settings where settlers could gossip and sip whiskey while waiting. *Photo courtesy of Jane Simon Ammeson*

traffic into the parking lot of the Graue Mill, built in 1852 by Frederick Graue in what was then Fullersburg, Illinois. Passing under the stone bridge along Salt Creek, I walk up the stairs toward the back of the mill and watch the waterwheel churning streams of water into the millrace. Families are picnicking here, while others are fishing along the creek. The beautifully bucolic spot is one of only two operating waterwheel gristmills in Illinois and one of only three authenticated Underground Railroad stations in the state. Lincoln is known to have visited the mill during a trip from Chicago to Springfield. Picture-perfect, totally restored, and surrounded by lawns and gardens, the two-story brick and limestone building definitely is a step back in time.

Facing, Abraham Lincoln stopped by Graue Mill on his way from Chicago to Springfield. In 1981, Graue Mill was recognized as an Illinois Historic Mechanical Engineering Landmark by the American Society of Mechanical Engineers. It's the only gristmill so designated on a national or local level and is representative of an important technology and era in the history of America. *Photo courtesy of Jane Simon Ammeson*

HONORING LINCOLN IN THE WINDY CITY

There are six outdoor statues of Lincoln in Chicago, and one of the finest was created by sculptor Augustus Saint-Gaudens using the 1860 life mask of Lincoln made by Chicago sculptor Leonard Volk. Titled *Abraham Lincoln: The Man*, it was dedicated on October 22, 1887, in front of thousands of people and stands in Lincoln Park at the intersection of Clark Street and North Avenue. Replicas of this work also stand outside London's Westminster Abbey and in Mexico City.

THE TREMONT HOUSE

I was born and raised near Chicago and spent many weekends in the city, but I've never thought of it as a Lincoln type of place. I was wrong. Lincoln was here frequently, often staying at the Tremont House, which served as his campaign headquarters during the presidential election in 1860. In 1859, when on an inspection tour of the Illinois Central Railroad, he had brought his young son Willie, who wrote about the experience to his friend Henry Lemann: "This town is a very beautiful place. . . . Me and father have a nice little room to ourselves. . . . We have two little pitchers on a washstand. The smallest one for me the largest one for father. We have two little towels on a top of both pitchers. The smallest one for me, the largest one for father."

During the 1860 presidential convention, Chicago hotels overflowed, and the Tremont was extremely busy with guests consuming 5,220 pounds of beef, 1,620 pounds of ham, 1,229 pounds of chicken, 880 pairs of pigeons, 1,400 pounds of fresh fish, 166 bushels of potatoes, 2,102 dozen eggs, 1,630 gallons of milk, 1,260 pounds of butter, and 1,380 pounds of sugar.

Established in 1836, the very first Tremont House, Chicago's first hotel, stood on the northwest corner of Dearborn and Lake in the Chicago Loop. Destroyed by fire in 1839, the Tremont Hotel was rebuilt on the southeast corner of the same intersection, where it stood until 1849, when it too burned.

The third Tremont House, constructed in 1850 at the same site as the second, was considered the leading hotel in the West. The Tremont was a landmark for several important political events of the mid-nineteenth century. Both Abraham Lincoln and Stephen Douglas announced their campaign for the senate from the Tremont balcony, leading to the famous Lincoln-Douglas debates of 1858.

File this under "not again," but in 1871, the Tremont House burned down during the Great Chicago Fire. A fourth Tremont was built two years later. In 1902, it was purchased by Northwestern University and used for their law, dental, and business schools. As for the Tremont Hotel, it became part of Chicago's history, and the Tremont name faded into memory for decades until John Coleman, a Chicago merchant banker, bought the current location in 1976, remodeled it, and reopened it as the Tremont Hotel—preserving the Lincoln connection.

Real Lincoln aficionados should also stop at Chicago's Abraham Lincoln Book Shop, which since 1938 has specialized in Lincolniana, material related to the Civil War, and material related to US presidents.

PLACES TO VISIT

Abraham Lincoln Book Shop
824 West Superior Street, Suite 100
Chicago, IL
(312) 944-3085
https://www.alincolnbookshop.com

Abraham Lincoln: The Man Statue
Lincoln Park
Intersection of Clark Street and North Avenue
Chicago, IL

Abraham Lincoln Watermelon Monument
Near the corner of Broadway and Sangamon Streets
Lincoln, IL
(217) 735-2815

Alton City Cemetery
Fifth Street and Monument Avenue
Alton, IL

Ann Mayes Rutledge Gravesite
Oakland Cemetery
17536 Oakland Terrace Avenue
Petersburg, IL 62675
(217) 632-3022

Apple River Fort State Historic Site
311 East Myrtle Street
Elizabeth, IL
http://www.appleriverfort.org

Belvedere Mansion and Gardens
1008 Park Avenue
Galena, IL
(815) 777-0747
http://www.belvederemansionandgardens.com

Bryant Cottage
146 Wilson Street
Bement, IL
(217) 678-8184
https://www.facebook.com/BryantCottageStateHistoricSite

Cahokia Courthouse
107 Elm Street
Cahokia, IL
(618) 332-1782

Clayville Historical Site
12828 State Route 125
Pleasant Plains, IL
(217) 572-4984
http://www.clayville.org/

Crenshaw Mansion
Off Route 1
Equality, IL 62934

DeSoto House
230 South Main Street
Galena, IL
(800) 343-6562
https://www.desotohouse.com/hotel-history/

Galena Trolley Tours
314 South Main Street
Galena, IL
(815) 777-1248
http://www.galenatrolleys.com

Graue Mill
3800 York Road
Oak Brook, IL
(630) 655-2090
http://www.grauemill.org

Halfway Tavern
US Route 50, just east of Salem, IL
(618) 548-2222

John Wood Mansion
425 South 12th Street
Quincy, IL
(217) 222-1835
https://www.hsqac.org/tours-events/the-john-wood-mansion

Lincoln and Civil War Legacy Trail
https://www.enjoyillinois.com/explore/listing/lincoln-and
-civil-war-legacy-trail

Lincoln-Douglas Debate Interpretative Center
128 North 5th Street
Quincy, IL
(217) 228-8696

Lincoln Douglas Debate Museum
126 East Street (enter at east end of the Coles County
Fairgrounds)
Charleston, IL
(217) 345-5650

Lincoln-Douglas Debate Plaza
Washington Park
4th and Main Streets
Quincy, IL
(217) 228-8696

Lincoln-Era Log Cabin Village
Bonansinga and Cedar Streets
Quincy, IL
(217) 223-7703
http://www.logcabinvillagequincyil.com

The Lincoln Log Cabin
402 South Lincoln Highway
Lerna, IL
(217) 345-1845
http://www.lincolnlogcabin.org

Lincoln Memorial Park
521 North Main Street
Jonesboro, IL
(618) 253-7114

Lincoln's New Salem State Historic Site
5588 History Lane
Petersburg, IL
(217) 632-4000
http://www.lincolnsnewsalem.com

Lincoln Trail Homestead State Park
705 Spitler Park Drive
Mt. Zion, IL
(217) 864-3121
https://www.dnr.illinois.gov/Parks/Pages
/LincolnTrailHomestead.aspx

Mt. Pulaski Courthouse State Historic Site
113 South Washington Street
Mt. Pulaski, IL
(217) 782-4836
https://www2.illinois.gov/dnrhistoric/Experience/Sites
/Central/Pages/Mount-Pulaski.aspx

The Newberry
60 West Walton Street
Chicago, IL
(312) 943-9090
https://www.newberry.org

Old Market House
123 North Commerce Street
Galena, IL 61036
(815) 777-3310

The Pierre Menard Home State Historic Site
4230 Kaskaskia Street
Ellis Grove, IL
(618) 859-3031
http://www.greatriverroad.com/stegen/randattract
/menard.htm

Dr. Richard Eells House
415 Jersey Street
Quincy, IL
(217) 223-1800
https://www.nps.gov/nr/travel/underground/il3.htm

Second Debate
114 East Douglas Street
Freeport, IL
(800) 369-2955
https://www.nps.gov/liho/learn/historyculture/debate2.htm

Ulysses S. Grant Home
500 Bouthillier Street
Galena, IL
(815) 777-3310
http://www.granthome.com

Vandalia State House State Historic Site
315 West Gallatin Street
Vandalia, IL
(618) 283-1161

The Washburne House Historical Site
908 Third Street
Galena, IL
(815) 777-3310
http://www.granthome.com/washburnehouse2.htm

7

OTHER PLACES
ALONG THE WAY

LOUISVILLE

In 1841 you and I had together a tedious low-water trip, on a Steam Boat from Louisville to St. Louis. You may remember, as I well do, that from Louisville to the mouth of the Ohio, there were, on board, ten or a dozen slaves, shackled together with irons. That sight was a continued torment to me; and I see something like it every time I touch the Ohio, or any other slave-border . . . I was losing interest in politics, when the repeal of the Missouri Compromise aroused me again. (Abraham Lincoln to his good friend, Joshua Speed, Springfield, Illinois, August 24, 1855)

Joshua Speed and Lincoln departed on their 1841 trip to St. Louis near what is now the Lincoln Memorial at Waterfront Park, located in the wide expanse of green running along the Ohio River in downtown Louisville. That's also likely the spot where Speed greeted Lincoln when he arrived to visit his friend in August of that year after a breakup with Mary Todd. Now

Abraham Lincoln traveled by boat to Louisville, where he and his friend Joshua Speed took another trip down the Ohio River. Visitors can travel like Lincoln aboard the *Belle of Louisville*, a refurbished paddlewheel boat built in 1915. *Photo courtesy of Louisville Convention & Visitors Bureau*

a stop on the Kentucky Lincoln Trail, the memorial features a twelve-foot statue of Lincoln sitting on a rock and looking out across the river to Indiana, four stone sculptures highlighting scenes of Lincoln's lifelong ties to Kentucky, and a granite amphitheater etched with famous Lincoln quotes that explain his values and beliefs. Designed by the landscape architectural firm Hargreaves Associates, the park is a beautiful setting that includes plantings of several types of trees known to be among Lincoln's favorites.

It's just a short walk from Waterfront Park to the towering Galt House, a downtown Louisville icon with a history harking back to Abraham Lincoln. The original Galt House, a sixty-room hotel on the northeast corner of Second and Main Streets, first opened in 1835. The owner was the wonderfully named Colonel Ariss Throckmorton. Over the years many notables would stay at the Galt, including not only Abraham Lincoln but also General Ulysses S. Grant, who met there with General William

Tecumseh Sherman to plan the historic March to the Sea. The food here, in a hotel known for refinement and grace, would be much more sophisticated fare than what young Lincoln had been raised on.

The building burned down in 1865, but the Galt House was rebuilt and opened four years later on the corner of First and Main Streets. Though the new Galt initially flourished, by 1919 it was derelict, and two years later, after going out of business, it was torn down. But the idea of a grand Galt Hotel rising above the Ohio River in the city's downtown persisted, and more than a half century later, a twenty-five-story, 1,290-room Galt House was built again on the corner of First and Main Streets. Sure, it's a different hotel from the one Lincoln stayed in, but it is still a tie to his Midwest history, as is the Ohio River, which the Galt House overlooks.

HISTORIC FARMINGTON PLANTATION: A HAVEN FOR THE HEARTBROKEN

Lincoln took the river trip to Louisville in 1841 to visit Joshua Speed, who had been a close friend in Springfield, after breaking his engagement with Mary Todd. In 1840, Speed's father had passed away, and in January of 1841 Joshua returned to the Farmington Plantation to help his mother manage the estate. This unfortunate turn of events turned out to be very fortunate for Lincoln. "When Mary and Abe broke off their engagement, Lincoln was really morose," says Terry Pyles, a docent at Farmington. "Joshua invited Lincoln to stay here." As we all know, Lincoln was prone to melancholy, and some believe the three-week visit at Farmington may have saved his life.

Speed was at the wharf to meet Lincoln when his steamboat docked, and for almost the entire month of August 1841, Lincoln was able to spend time with his good friend and his family and restore his good spirits. There's another reason to believe the

Lincoln visited Farmington, the Federal-style home of his good friend
Joshua Speed, for a much-needed respite after breaking his engagement to
Mary Todd. *Photo courtesy of Louisville Convention & Visitors Bureau*

visit was important to Lincoln: while he was at Farmington he
spent long hours discussing law with Joshua's brother James
Speed, who he would later select for his attorney general.

The Farmington Plantation consisted of a Federal-style
home built in 1816 by John Speed and his wife, Lucy, a 550-
acre hemp farm, and over fifty slaves. While not confirmed, it's
widely believed that Thomas Jefferson designed the plans for
the Speed house. Recipes for the foods Lincoln may have eaten
while living with the family have been researched and recreated
in the cookbook *Speed Family Heritage Recipes: Commemorating
the 200th Anniversary of Farmington Historic Plantation* edited
by Susan E. Lindsey, sales of which benefit the restored plantation. The mansion is now a house museum, and the farm
is again growing hemp, as the Speeds did all those years ago.
Farmington is also only fifteen minutes Louisville's Waterfront

Park and often hosts culinary events, like their famous Derby Day Breakfast and a recent heirloom dinner featuring foods from the cookbook.

CINCINNATI

In September 1855, Lincoln spent about a week in Cincinnati, but as he was leaving, he told his hostess, Mrs. William M. Dickson, who was a cousin of Mary's: "You have made my stay most agreeable, and I am a thousand times obligated to you; but in reply to your request for me to come again, I must say to you, I never expect to be in Cincinnati again. I have nothing against the city, but things have so happened here as to make it undesirable for me ever to return."

So, what happened to Lincoln during his week in this Ohio River city to make him not want to come back? It seems that Lincoln was involved in a case with a lawyer named Edwin M. Stanton called *McCormic v. Manny*, which he thought would be tried in Springfield but was moved to Cincinnati. Stanton and the other eastern lawyers who were involved in the case were less than impressed with Lincoln—mostly, it seems, because of his odd looks but probably also because he wasn't as polished or refined. Though Lincoln was in the courtroom during the proceedings the other lawyers ignored him; they threw his brief in the trash, and he wasn't allowed to participate in any aspect of trying the case. Later, when Lincoln was to try a case in front of the Supreme Court in Washington, DC, Stanton is said to have stated, "If that giraffe appears in the case, I'll throw up my brief."

Seven years later, when President Lincoln had to select a secretary of war, he was told the best man for the job was Stanton but also that Stanton wouldn't be recommended for the position because of his disrespectful behavior toward the president. Lincoln agreed that was true. But he said he wanted the best man for the job. Stanton got it.

While in Cincinnati for that case, Lincoln visited the estate of Nicholas Longworth, now the Taft Museum, named after the brother of President Taft who once owned it. Built about 1820 for Martin Baum, it is the oldest domestic wooden structure in situ locally and is considered one of the best examples of Federal architecture in the Palladian style in the United States. The building is a national historic landmark. While Lincoln was wandering in the gardens, he accidentally mistook the owner—who was weeding in old clothing—for the gardener and asked if his master allowed visitors. Upon realizing his mistake, Lincoln apologized, and Longworth told him it happened a lot and sometimes he got tipped as much as a quarter, adding, "I might say that it's the only really honest money I ever make, having been by profession a lawyer." Proving that lawyer jokes are nothing new.

OFF THE BEATEN PATH IN OHIO

Lincoln supped and stayed at the Buxton Inn in lovely Granville, Ohio, which has another interesting connection to a US president. At the time the inn was built in 1812 by Orin Granger, it had a stagecoach court, a dining room, and a ballroom. Granger's good friend General William Henry Harrison, soon to be elected the ninth president of the United States, visited the inn one night where he imbibed way too much, left the dining room, found his horse, and rode it into the lobby and upstairs to a second-floor bedroom. Here, Harrison announced, his horse would spend the night. Others had a different take on the horse's sleeping quarters, and, blindfolding the equine, led him back downstairs.

Although it's not been recorded (it's certainly possible) that Lincoln dined at the Golden Lamb in Lebanon, Ohio, he may have influenced it in another way. In 1863 he proclaimed the fourth Thursday of November a national holiday. The inn has served meals on Thanksgiving every year since then, in the

Although the building has changed considerably over the years, the central brick structure of the Golden Lamb Inn in Lebanon, Ohio, recently celebrated its two hundredth birthday. *Photo courtesy of the Golden Lamb*

same dining room and in the same building where they'll serve it this year. That building, the central brick structure of the inn, recently celebrated its two hundredth birthday, having opened in 1816. Though it's been added to many times since, the inn's historic core includes the main dining room and some of the guest rooms. The inn's beginnings are even older, starting when Jonas Seaman spent four dollars on a license to open a log-cabin tavern under the sign of a golden lamb (because literacy wasn't common, signs with images were used instead).

PLACES TO VISIT

Belle of Louisville
401 West River Rd
Louisville, KY
(502) 574-2992
http://www.belleoflouisville.org

The Buxton Inn
313 East Broadway
Granville, OH
(740) 587-0001
https://www.buxtoninn.com

Farmington Historic Plantation
3033 Bardstown Road
Louisville, KY
(502) 452-9920
https://farmingtonhistoricplantation.org

Galt House
140 North Fourth Street
Louisville, KY
(502) 589-5200; (800) THE-GALT
https://www.galthouse.com

Golden Lamb
27 South Broadway
Lebanon, KY
(513) 932-5065
https://www.goldenlamb.com

Lincoln Memorial at Waterfront Park
401 River Road, just east of the Big Four Bridge
Louisville, KY
(502) 574-3768
https://louisvillewaterfront.com

ENDINGS

FINAL GOODBYES IN COLES COUNTY

In 1858, Lincoln traveled to Charleston in Coles County, a city in east-central Illinois, to participate in the fourth Lincoln-Douglas debate (its history can be viewed at the Lincoln Douglas Debate Museum there), but it wasn't the first or last time he'd visit here. Lincoln's work as a lawyer often brought him to Coles County, and Coles County was where his father, stepmother, and other members of his family lived.

Over the years, Lincoln tried many cases in Coles County—tagline "Buckle on the Corn Belt"—and according to Charles H. Coleman in his book *Abraham Lincoln and Coles County, Illinois*, Abraham Lincoln's court win/loss record in Coles County was above average. Of his twenty-four cases there, twenty-two were civil cases of a large variety, and two were criminal. When representing the plaintiff, Lincoln won nine and lost two. When representing the defendant, he won four cases and lost five. In both of his criminal cases, both defendants lost, although he got pardons for both.

Lincoln was described as always being well prepared and doing his share of the work when working with a partner. Probably his most famous case took place in October 1847 in Charleston in a case titled *Matson v. Ashmore et al. for the use of Bryant.* Lincoln was just two weeks away from leaving for Congress when the case went to trial, and for the man who would become known as the Great Emancipator, he was on the wrong side of the case. Lincoln's client Robert Matson was a slave owner in Kentucky who also held land in Illinois. On the other side was Anthony Bryant, formerly a slave owned by Matson, and his wife, Jane, and their children, who were still enslaved. The argument, simply put—but more complex because of the laws back then—was that the rest of the Bryant family should be freed because they were in Illinois, a free state. Matson disagreed, sending one of the Bryant's children back to Kentucky. Matson filed suit. Lincoln was up against a friend who was representing Bryant. In this case we were rooting against Lincoln, who lost. The Bryants went free.

As for the Lincoln family, after moving from Decatur, Tom Lincoln moved again and again. But everything has to end sometime, and after moving from the Decatur area to three more failed farms in Coles County, Sarah and Tom settled in an area on the Embarras River called Goosenest Prairie. Their home, purchased by Abe, was known as a saddleback-style log cabin with two rooms and a loft accessible by ladder. They needed the space because at times, as seemed so common in pioneer days, as many as eighteen people lived in the cabin, including Abe's stepbrother John Johnston and his sister and stepsisters, Sarah, Elizabeth, and Matilda, along with their families.

Though Lincoln practiced law frequently in Charleston, he visited his father and stepmother only every year or so. When Thomas was dying, Lincoln didn't visit despite letters from family members urging him to do so, including one from his stepbrother, John, to which Lincoln replied, "Say to him that if

The Lincoln Log Cabin State Historic Site near Lerna, the site of the last farm belonging to Thomas and Sarah Bush Lincoln. *Photo courtesy of Wikimedia*

we could meet now, it is doubtful whether it would not be more painful than pleasant." He was dutiful in other ways, though, sending money to help sustain the family and keep Sarah on her land after Thomas died in 1851. He also sent money to his step-brother John Johnston, who seemed to be allergic to work.

The Lincoln Log Cabin State Historical Site near Lerna, the site of the last farm belonging to the Lincolns, showcases the agricultural practices of 1840s Illinois, giving visitors a chance to learn about farm life back then. A replica of the cabin is also on site, the original having been disassembled and shipped to Chicago for the World's Columbian Exposition. Somehow it got lost afterwards, and historians surmise it might have been burned for firewood.

The eighty-six-acre Lincoln Log Cabin State Historic Site is a busy place with approximately ten acres of heritage crops that would have been grown back then, a hay field, and teams of working oxen and horses as well as sheep. The pigs raised there

LINCOLN ROAD TRIP

are similar to the razorback hogs of Lincoln's day, which provided the meat served in homes and taverns of the time. Other historic replicas of farm structures include a log smokehouse, a well, a root cellar, hog pens and shelters, a chicken house, a sheep pen, orchards, and gardens. Part of the experience involves costumed interpreters cultivating fields, caring for the animals, and performing the never-ending domestic chores of that era. The historic reenactment is so authentic that the interpreters—who represent a host of characters who might be found in the area back then, including traveling preachers, a family of pioneers, an itinerant tinker, and even Lincoln himself—speak in period dialogue and profess to know "nothing" about life after 1845. This is the life Lincoln escaped.

For about a year or so, Dennis and Sarah Hanks's daughter Harriet also tried to escape, moving in with Abe and Mary Lincoln in Springfield, which today is about an hour-and-a-half drive from Charleston. She was the only Coles County relative that we know of to visit the Lincolns in Springfield. In fact, Mary never even met any of her husband's other relatives. According to presidential historian Feather Foster Schwartz writing on her Presidential History Blog, Harriet, who was in her late teens, wanted an education. Mary Todd Lincoln needed help with her family as she was often alone, with her husband on the road so much. The deal was that Harriet would attend school in Springfield, stay with the Lincolns, and help Mary with the childcare and the housework. It didn't work out. Why? Mary was a Todd, and Harriet, besides being poor, had "limited breeding." To a socialite (read snob) like Mary, that meant Harriet was a servant, while the teen saw herself as family. Ironically, Mary's attitude toward others of lesser social standing seems similar to that of the stepmother she so disliked.

Though he didn't come see his dying father, Lincoln traveled to Coles County to say goodbye to his step-mother Sarah Bush Lincoln on his way to Washington, DC, as president-elect of the United States. Sarah was seventy-two years old when Lincoln visited on January 31, 1861, and staying at the home of her daughter and son-in-law, Matilda and Reuben Moore, a mile north of Goosenest Prairie in the former village of Farmington. Residents and neighbors turned out for a big dinner in honor of Lincoln's visit and Lincoln and his stepmother rode out to Shiloh Cemetery to visit Thomas Lincoln's grave.

And then it came time for Lincoln to leave to catch a train for Springfield. Sarah, it is said, believed it would be the last time she would see her stepson, and it wasn't because of her advanced age. A letter from August Chapman included in the book *Herndon's Informants*, recalls that Sarah had a premonition that something tragic would happen to her stepson: "She embraced him when they parted and said she would never be permitted to see him again, that she felt his enemies would assassinate him. He replied, 'No, no, Mama (he always called her Mama) they will not do that. Trust in the Lord and all will be well. We will see each other again.'"

Several years later, when Herndon was collecting his stories about Lincoln, Johnston, who would die on April 12, 1869, described her stepson thus: "He was dutiful to me always. I think he loved me truly. I had a son, John, who was raised with Abe. Both were good boys; but I must say, both now being dead, that Abe was the best boy I ever saw, or expect to see. I wish I had died when my husband died. I did not want Abe to run for President; did not want him elected; was afraid somehow, felt in my heart; and when he came down to see me, after he was elected President, I still felt that something told me that something would befall Abe, and that I should see him no more."

Many historians suppose that Sarah Bush had turned down Thomas Lincoln's first proposal, before she married her husband and he married Nancy Hanks, because she believed that he would never amount to much. When he returned as a widower and asked her to marry, the theory goes, he made his farm and life in Little Pigeon Creek sound much more prosperous and grand than it was. She married him believing that and instead found a filthy, poor home with little furniture and three (remember, Dennis was there too) wild, dirty, and unschooled children. But she didn't leave or sulk. Instead, newly married Sarah Lincoln saw her duty, and she fulfilled it. She made a home for the family, and she raised a future president.

AFTER MR. LINCOLN: MARY'S RESTLESS LIFE

After her husband's death in 1865, Mary Todd Lincoln left Washington and moved to Chicago where she and her son Tad stayed for a time at the Tremont House and then at the Hyde Park Hotel. In 1866 she purchased a home at 375 W. Washington in Chicago with views in both directions from her parlor. The house, which is no longer standing, was located between Willard (later known as Ann) and Elizabeth Streets. Like street names, street numbers also change; 375 was the address when Mary lived there but no longer matches the location of the house. The neighborhood was one of the city's most fashionable places in the 1860s. Like many city streets, Washington had a wooden sidewalk—many of those would be destroyed by the Chicago Fire in 1871.

For a short time, mother and son established a life for themselves. Mary worshipped at the Third Presbyterian Church at Washington and Carpenter Streets, and Tad attended Brown School on Warren Avenue between Page and Wood Streets and Sunday school at what was the old First Congregational Church at Washington and Green Streets. In May 1867 Mary rented out the Washington Street house and moved to the Clifton House at the southeast corner of Wabash and Madison. Tad went to school at the Chicago Academy. That same year, they moved back to Washington Street, living at 340 in a house almost opposite the 13-acre Union Park.

In 1868 Mary moved back to the Clifton House and then went to Europe for a few years. Upon returning to Chicago in May 1871, she and Tad lived with Mary's eldest son Robert at his home at 653 Wabash Avenue. But that didn't last long. She and

Tad were soon back at the Clifton House where Tad would die on July 15, 1871. Mary went back to Robert's, and then next came a trip to health spas in Wisconsin, Florida, and Canada. In 1874 Mary was living at the Grand Pacific Hotel. On April 6, 1874, she sold her old home on Washington Street.

MARY ON HER OWN

Mary Todd Lincoln was staying at Robert Lincoln's house on Wabash when the Chicago Fire began on October 8, 1871. Robert's house was one block south and two blocks east of the burnt area. He was home with his mother when the fire started. Robert ran out to his law office at 154 Lake Street, in the Marine Bank Building, to try to save what he could . . . including some of his father's letters. The law office was burnt to the ground.

Because of all the smoke the neighborhood panicked and rushed to the lakefront to avoid the smoke and fire burning just a block away. It's unclear if Mary stayed at home or if she when with neighbors to the lakefront. Both Mary and Robert survived as did Robert's house. (Digital Research Library of Illinois History Journal, "Mary Todd Lincoln–In the Midst of the 1871 Great Chicago Fire")

Although she survived her husband by almost two decades, Mary never seemed to find peace. Her health was poor, and looking back at her symptoms, it's thought she suffered from depression, anxiety, and paranoia as well as migraine headaches and possibly even diabetes. Mary was always interested in spiritualism (as was Lincoln), but after his death she became even more so. She had her portrait taken by William H. Mumler, a famous spiritual photographer, and the resulting photo purported to show Mary with a ghostly Lincoln standing behind her. A scandal ensued when it was discovered the photo was fake. Mumler was tried and acquitted for fraud. Mary, caught in this maelstrom of bad publicity, took another emotional hit.

There were other scandals as well. In 1866, Congress investigated her because of allegations she had taken items such as china and silverware when leaving the White House. Nothing was proven but it was, as one can imagine, humiliating for the already unstable and still grieving mother and widow.

Only one of Mary's four sons outlived her, and after the death of her third son, her life spiraled further down into depression. After some political wrangling, Mary eventually received an increase in her pension from $3,000 to $5000 a year (almost $90,000 today). But even when Lincoln was alive she overspent, and after his death she quickly ran out of money. She even tried selling some of her high priced possessions under the name of Mrs. Clarke but her real name was soon discovered, causing her further embarrassment. Another blow to her esteem occurred when William Herndon, Lincoln's law partner, took the stance that the only true love in the president's life had been Ann Rutledge, traveled around giving his Lincoln/Rutledge speech, and wrote about the romance in his book. Despite Robert's attempts to keep his mother from finding out about it, Mary heard what Herndon was doing and was angry with him until she died. It wasn't exactly the kind of thing any woman would want said about her deceased husband.

MORE WRETCHED LUCK: IT REALLY WAS CRUMMY BEING MARY

Case is one of mental impairment which probably dates back to the murder of President Lincoln—More pronounced since the death of her son, but especially aggravated during the last 2 months. (A notation from the May 20, 1875, ledger of the Bellevue Place, where Mary Lincoln was held for several months after being declared insane.)

With three sons dead and one husband murdered in front of her, Mary's moorings from reality seemed to loosen, and her only remaining son, Robert, grew increasingly worried about his mother.

KEEPING MARY SAFE

Robert kept asking his mother to live with him after she returned from Florida. When she wouldn't do so, he rented a room next to hers at the Grand Pacific Hotel where she had checked in. He also hired Pinkerton detectives to follow her because of her erratic behavior, and paid the hotel staff to keep tabs on her as well.

She was having what we might consider now to be paranoid delusions—thinking someone on a train had poisoned her coffee. Her interest in the occult increased, and she visited more and more clairvoyants. She also walked the streets of the city with $56,000 ($1,185,847.19 today) sewn into her petticoats. There were other incidents, such as when a half-dressed Mary tried to enter the elevator at her hotel thinking it was a bathroom, and, as Robert and the staff attempted to get her back to her room, shouted that her son was trying to kill her.

There is another factor to consider when writing about Mary's mental status. In July 1862, just a year after Willie's death, Mary was riding alone in a carriage when the driver's seat snapped, the horses spooked, and Mary was thrown from the carriage, hitting her head on a rock. She was bleeding badly and later developed a brain infection. It was later discovered the seat had been loosened, possibly to harm the president. Could the accident and resulting infection have caused sometime type of brain trauma?

On May 19, 1875, she opened her hotel room door thinking she was accepting a delivery of lace curtains. The delivery boy was there but so were three men including Leonard Swett, an old family friend and Chicago attorney who had supported Abraham Lincoln's run for the presidency. They needed to take her into custody for her own good, Swett told Mary, and would handcuff her to do so if need be, though he hoped she would go willingly. She agreed and tearfully asked to see Robert. She didn't know yet that he had been accumulating evidence against her, even while she was still in Florida.

Robert was waiting at the Cook County Courthouse, having petitioned to have her committed to a mental institution as a danger to herself. After a three-hour trial, which began the afternoon she was taken from her apartment, it took the jury ten minutes to come to a verdict. Mary was sent to Bellevue Insane Asylum in Batavia, Illinois, which, according to an advertisement, was "For the Insane of the Private Class." She then twice attempted suicide by taking laudanum and camphor. Fortunately, her druggist, suspecting she was suicidal, had given her a placebo.

Bellevue Place is now an apartment building, but Mary's history there can be found at the Batavia's Depot Museum, where displays include the bed and dresser she used at Bellevue and the hospital ledger with notes about her moods, diagnosis, and activities.

> It does not appear that God is good, to have placed me here. I endeavor to read my Bible and offer up my petitions three times a day. But my afflicted heart fails me and my voice often falters in prayer. I have worshiped my son and no unpleasant word ever passed between us, yet I cannot understand why I should have been brought out here. (Letter written by Mary Todd Lincoln during her stay at Bellevue Place in Batavia, Illinois, from Jason Emerson, *The Madness of Mary Lincoln*, 165)

But Mary persevered, and within three months, with the support of powerful friends and against the advice of Bellevue Place's owner, she was released. Throughout her remaining days, Mary lived with her sister Elizabeth Edwards in Springfield, Illinois; abroad in Europe with her surviving son, Robert; and in Chicago. Her final days were spent again with Elizabeth Edwards; she died in 1882 at age sixty-three, her sight almost gone.

PLACES TO VISIT

Batavia Historical Society
155 Houston Street
Batavia, IL
(630) 406-5274
http://www.bataviahistoricalsociety.org

Bellevue Place
333 South Jefferson Street
Batavia, IL

Lincoln Douglas Debate Museum
126 East Street (enter at east end of the Coles County
Fairgrounds)
Charleston, IL
(217) 345-5650

The Lincoln Log Cabin State Historic Site
402 South Lincoln Highway
Lerna, IL
(217) 345-1845
http://www.lincolnlogcabin.org

Selected Bibliography

Baker, Jean H. *Mary Todd Lincoln: A Biography*. New York: W.W. Norton, 1986.

Basler, Roy P., ed. *Collected Works of Abraham Lincoln*. Vol. 8. New Brunswick, NJ: Rutgers University Press, 1953.

Bernstein, Arnie. *The Hoofs and Guns of the Storm: Chicago's Civil War Connections*. Chicago: Lake Claremont Press, 2003.

Beveridge, Albert J. *Abraham Lincoln: 1808 to 1859*. 2 vols. Boston: Houghton Mifflin, 1928.

Bryan, William S., and Robert Rose. *A History of the Pioneer Families of Missouri, with Numerous Sketches, Anecdotes, Adventures, Etc., Relating to Early Days in Missouri*. St. Louis, MO: Bryan, Brand & Co, 1876. Facsimile of the first edition. Baltimore, MD: Genealogical Publishing, 1977.

Burlingame, Michael. *Abraham Lincoln: A Life*. Baltimore, MD: Johns Hopkins University Press, 2012.

Burlingame, Michael. *The Inner World of Abraham Lincoln*. Urbana: University of Illinois Press, 1994.

Coleman, Charles H. *Abraham Lincoln and Coles County, Illinois*. New Brunswick, NJ: Scarecrow Press, 1955.

Coon, Diane Perrine. "Early African American Education in Shelby County Kentucky." HistorybyPerrine.com, November 21, 2014. http://www.historybyperrine.com/early-african-american-education-shelby-county-kentucky/.

Digital Research Library of Illinois History Journal, "Mary Todd Lincoln– In the Midst of the 1871 Great Chicago Fire." https://drloihjournal.blogspot.com/2016/11/mary-todd-lincoln-in-midst-of-chicago.html.

Eighmey, Rae Katherine. *Abraham Lincoln in the Kitchen: A Culinary View of Lincoln's Life and Times*. Washington, DC: Smithsonian Books, 2013.

Ehrmann, Bess V. *The Missing Chapter in the Life of Abraham Lincoln: A number of articles, episodes, photographs, pen and ink sketches concerning the life of Abraham Lincoln in Spencer County, Indiana, between1816–1830 and 1844*. Chicago: Walter M. Hill, 1938.

Ellison, Betty Boles. *The True Mary Todd Lincoln: A Biography*. Jefferson, NC: McFarland, 2014.

Emerson, Jason. *The Madness of Mary Lincoln*. Carbondale: Southern Illinois University Press, 2007.

Fernandez, Megan. "Lincoln Like Me." Indianapolis Monthly, October 25, 2012.

Gannett, Lewis. "The Ann Rutledge Story: Case Closed?" *Journal of the Abraham Lincoln Association* 31, no. 2 (Summer 2010): 21–60. https://quod.lib .umich.edu/cgi/p/pod/dod-idx/ann-rutledge-story-case-closed .pdf?c=jala;idno=2629860.0031.205;format=pdf.

Grigsby, Susan. "About That Grigsby Tombstone That Calls Democrats Traitors." *Daily Kos*, July 11, 2014. https://www.dailykos.com/stories/2014 /7/11/1313379/-About-that-Grigsby-tombstone-that-calls-Democrats -Traitors.

Hamilton, Michelle L. *I Would Still Be Drowned in Tears: Spiritualism in Abraham Lincoln's White House*. LaMesa, CA: Vanderblumen Publications, 2013.

Helm, Katherine. *The True Story of Mary, Wife of Lincoln* [. . .]. New York: Harper and Brothers Publishers, 1928.

Herndon, William H. *Life of Lincoln*. Rockville, MD: Wildside Press, 2008.

Herndon, William H., and Jesse William Weik. *Herndon's Lincoln: The True Story of a Great Life* [. . .]. Chicago: Belford, Clarke, & Company, 1889.

Hevron Family Cookbook: One Hundred Seventy-Five Years of Recipes and Reflections. Self-published. Fourth Printing May 2003.

Historic Downtown Walking Tours. *https://www.visitlex.com/listing/historic -downtown-walking-tours/6390/*.

Howells, William Cooper. *Recollections of Life in Ohio, from 1813–1840 . . .* Cincinnati: Robert Clarke Company, 1895.

Illinois Department of Natural Resources. "When Salt Was Gold." *Outdoor Illinois* (October 2009): 11–13.

Imlay, Gilbert. *A Topographical Description of the Western Territory of North America*. London: J. Debrett, 1797.

Jones, Dorothy Darnall. *Emilie Pariet Todd Helm: Abraham Lincoln's "Little Sister."* Coopersburg, PA: Deer Trail Publications, 2007.

Keckley, Elizabeth. *Behind the Scenes*. London, UK: Partridge and Oakey, 1868.

Kentucky Historical Society. "Kentucky's Abraham Lincoln: Abraham Lincoln Pleads His Own Case." Accessed September 17, 2018. http://www.lrc .ky.gov/record/Moments08RS/15_web_leg_moments.htm.

Lincoln, Abraham. "Letter to John D. Johnston, January 2 [?], 1851." In *The Complete Works of Abraham Lincoln*, vol. 2, new and enlarged ed., edited by John G. Nicolay and John Hay, 144–46. New York: Francis D. Tandy Company, 1905.

Lovell, Daryl, Ellen Winkler Rexing, and the History Book Committee. *Dale, Indiana 1843–1993*. Dale, IN: Lincoln Heritage Public Library, 1993.

Mazrim, Robert. *The Sangamo Frontier: History and Archaeology in the Shadow of Lincoln*. Chicago: University of Chicago Press, 2006.

McCreary, Donna D. *Lincoln's Table: A President's Culinary Journey from Cabin to Cosmopolitan*. 2nd ed. Charlestown, IN: Lincoln Presentations, 2008.

Morgan, Arthur E. "New Light on Lincoln's Boyhood." *Atlantic*, February 1920. https://www.theatlantic.com/past/docs/politics/presiden/morglin .htm.

Murr, J. Edward. 1918. "Lincoln in Indiana." *Indiana Magazine of History*
  (1918): 13–75. Retrieved from https://scholarworks.iu.edu/journals
  /index.php/imh/article/view/6069.

Musgrave, Jon. *Slaves, Salt, Sex & Mr. Crenshaw: The Real Story of the Old
  Slave House and America's Reverse Underground R.R.* Marion, IL:
  IllinoisHistory.com, 2005.

New-England Farmer and Horticultural Register, vol. 24. "Henry Clay's Farm."
  Boston: Joseph Breck and Company, 1846, 89.

Peachee, Carol. *Straight Bourbon: Distilling the Industry's Heritage.* Bloomington: Indiana University Press, 2017.

Power, John Carroll. *Early Settlers of Sangamon County.* Springfield, IL:
  Edwin A. Wilson & Co., 1876. https://archive.org/details/historyofearly
  seoopowe.

Robinson, Dr. H. E. "Lincoln, Hanks and Boone Families: Some Genealogical Notes Illustrating Their Connection." Reprinted from *Missouri Historical Review* 1, no. 1 (October 1906): 72–84. https://archive.org/details
  /lincolnhanksboonoorobi.

Sandburg, Carl. *Abraham Lincoln: The Prairie Years and the War Years.* One-
  vol. ed. San Diego: Harcourt, Inc., 1982.

Scripps, John Locke. *Life of Abraham Lincoln.* Bloomington: Indiana University Press, 1961.

Spraker, Hazel Atterbury. *The Boone Family: A Genealogical History of the Descendants of George and Mary Boone Who Came to America in 1717.* Rutland,
  VT: The Tuttle Company, 1922.

State Historical Society of Missouri. "Lincoln, Hanks and Boone Families:
  Some Genealogical Notes Illustrating Their Connections." *Missouri Historical Review* 1 (October 1906–July 1907): 71–84.

Tarbell, Ida M. 1895. "Abraham Lincoln: A Life." *McClure's Magazine* 6, no. 1,
  (December 1895–May 1896): 3–23.

Tarbell, Ida M. 1924. *In the Footsteps of the Lincolns.* New York: Harper &
  Brothers, 1924.

Van Stockum, Ron. "Squire Boone Chapter 7: Squire Boone's Painted Stone
  Station." *Sentinel News*, Thursday, September 10, 2009. https://www
  .sentinelnews.com/content/squire-boone-chapter-7-squire-boonersquos
  -painted-stone-station.

Veach, Michael. "Lincoln's Bourbon Legacy, or Did You Know Abe Was a
  Barkeep?" *LEO Weekly*, September 7, 2016. https://www.leoweekly
  .com/2016/09/lincolns-bourbon-legacy/.

Warren, Louis A. "President Lincoln's Interest in Catholic Institutions." *Lincoln Lore: Bulletin of the Lincoln National Life Foundation*, May 29, 1944.

Warren, Louis A. "The Shipley Ancestry of Lincoln's Mother." *Indiana Magazine of History* 29, No. 3, 1933, 202–12.

Weik, Jesse W. *The Real Lincoln: A Portrait.* Boston: Houghton Mifflin, 1922.

Wilson, Douglas L. *Honor's Voice: The Transformation of Abraham Lincoln.*
  New York: Alfred A. Knopf, 1998.

Wilson, Douglas L., and Rodney O. Davis, eds. *Herndon's Informants: Letters, Interviews, and Statements about Abraham Lincoln.* Urbana: University of Illinois Press, 1997.

Index of Place Names

INDEX OF PLACE NAMES

JANE SIMON AMMESON is a freelance writer and photographer who specializes in travel, food, and personalities. She writes frequently for newspapers, magazines, websites, and apps and is the author of 13 books, including *Hauntings of the Underground Railroad*, *Murders that Made Headlines*, and *How to Murder Your Wealthy Lovers and Get Away With It*.

A James Beard Foundation judge, as well as a member of the Society of American Travel Writers (SATW) and Midwest Travel Journalists Association (MTJA), Jane's home base is on the shores of Lake Michigan in southwest Michigan. Follow Jane on Facebook; Twitter (@HPAmmeson and @travelfoodIN); and on her blogs, *Will Travel for Food with Jane Ammeson* and *Travel/Food* (janeammeson.blog).